PAGAN RITUAL
The Path of the Priest and Priestess

By Anna Franklin

This first edition published by:
Lear Books
Windrush
High Tor West
Earl Shilton
Leics
LE9 7DN
UK

www.learbooks.co.uk

Cover design by Paul Mason

ISBN 978 0 9547534 6 7

Printed in England by Booksprint

CONTENTS

Chapter 1
WHAT IS RITUAL?

When you create within a sacred paradigm, you find a strange thing. You are communicating with, and being fed by, sources you know are within you, but have a much greater reflection somewhere else. You are in touch with something timeless." [a]

Elizabeth Fuller

The Oxford English Dictionary defines 'ritual' as "*a ceremonial act or series of acts, a prescribed method of procedure*". The word derives from Latin and relates to 'number' or 'counting', in the sense of the order that things should be done in, and this tells us the most fundamental thing about ritual.

Pagan ritual, whether it is an act or worship or magic, employs a specific series of stages, using symbolism and ceremony, to create a sacred place and state of consciousness whereby the participants are put in touch with forces outside themselves – the Gods. Step by step, we weave together the disparate threads of time, place and people using the beliefs, words, symbols, movements and intent of those involved to make the ritual pattern, a pattern by which we "*establish a link and cultivate a dialogue between the microcosm and the macrocosm*".[b] Ritual is a two way exchange between the microcosm (us and through us, our world) and the macrocosm (the greater Cosmos and the powers of the Gods).

The world-view of the majority of Pagans is holistic: all of the Cosmos, both manifest and unmanifest, even the gods and goddesses, are part of a single great whole. The divine is not separate from creation, but is manifest within it and within each of us; just as we are all contained within the divine spirit. We are indivisibly connected to everything else. Thus, the Pagan recognises his or her place in the Cosmos, not a stranger, or a separate being apart from it, but part of the living diversity in unity.[c]

We know that the material world we perceive with our five senses is only part of the whole; there are unseen Otherworlds overlapping our own, populated by gods and goddesses, non-incarnate adepts, nature spirits, elementals and wildfolk: embodiments of natural forces and energies: un-numbered conscious entities which are responsible for the functioning of the Cosmos. They have been given different names, faces and allotted assorted functions in sundry cultures around the world. We humans view them anthropomorphically in order to identify with them more closely as concepts we can easily grasp, but in truth they are not limited by the forms we give them, which merely reflect our own desires and fears: we only glimpse their essence.

It is said that there are two forms of magic, thaumaturgy which means 'the art of working wonders' harnessing natural forces to create effects, and theurgy which means 'divine work'. The latter is the approach of the Pagan, one that puts religion and magic hand in hand. Paganism is a religious path after all, but one which aims to develop the soul and the world by magical means. We recognise the existence of the creative forces of the Cosmos, and each person's right to approach the transcendental powers themselves without an intermediary, for as Dion Fortune said: "*The gods are alive in the minds of all of us, and it is up to us to open the channels of inspiration.*" [d]

However, ritual is something that many new Pagans have difficulty coming to terms with; after looking forward to their first ceremony, they are often left with a feeling of disappointment. I sometimes have probationers who are drawn to the ideology of the Craft, but say to me "*I don't like the rituals*" or "*I don't get anything out of the rituals*". They can be left unaffected while their fellow coven members are reeling under the impact of a powerful ceremony feeling divinely blessed and spiritually enlightened. They were all at the same event, so what was the difference? It may sound simplistic to say it, but you only get out of a ritual what you put in. If you merely observe and do not try to participate to your utmost capacity, then you will never be touched by ritual.

In order to work effective ritual, you need to understand why you are performing the ritual (its intent), you need to be fully prepared, purified and consecrated, able to understand the magical language (the symbolism and mythology) that the ritual employs, and you need to be capable of total concentration, able to focus your whole being on a single aim. You need to be able to relinquish your ego in order to become part of the group mind. Furthermore, the group needs to have effective techniques of opening up the channels to the Gods, and the individuals within the group the skill to receive that energy.

It has to be said that some covens, groves and moots are little more than communal meeting places, holding *ad hoc* festival celebrations that are little more than social events, paying lip-service to the relevant occasion. Such events are pale shadows of what rituals can be, merely touching the mental plane of ceremony, rather than connecting with the spiritual plane of ritual, and though it may satisfy and stimulate for a time, the effects of the ritual will not be profound, and will not last. It may sound very glamorous to call yourself a witch or a druid, but those titles have to be earned with study, commitment, time and effort in order to be able to move beyond the outer forms of worship. We live in a society that expects instant gratification, big rewards for little effort, and most resist the idea that self-discipline and hard work is necessary.

Those who give of themselves will receive blessings in return, stimulating experiences that extend their understanding and development far beyond the bounds of what may be achieved by study and meditation alone. Ritual is a powerful path to illumination; humankind, through ritual, gains access to the Cosmic consciousness.

Those who take readily to ritual are often Old Souls, celebrants of the mysteries in previous lifetimes whose past-life memories are stirred by ceremony. Newer souls take longer to come to terms with ritual.

However, some people can never work magical ritual at its deepest levels; it takes a special kind of person, what we call in the Craft a priest or priestess, a person who is willing undertake the training, to persevere when faced with failure, and who is able to find within themselves deep reserves of self-discipline, application and learning: an initiate. Not everyone has the strength of will and mental stamina to withstand the pressures of such a path.

Chapter 2
THE STEPS OF RITUAL

As Pagans, we hold a wide variety of rituals, private and public, seasonal and esbats, weddings, namings and funerals; rituals designed for magic, for transformation, for healing and to give thanks. There are many kinds of ritual structure used by modern Pagans. In its most basic form this might be:

1. Intent
2. Preparation
3. The building of sacred space
4. Invocation
5. The body of the ritual
6. Thanking the spirits invoked
7. Taking down the sacred space
8. Restoration of the site

In this chapter, I'll talk you through the steps of formulating a ritual and its execution in our tradition and ask you to think about each step described and how it might be applied to your own practices.

INTENT

The first and most important step in planning a ritual is to determine its intent: knowing exactly what you want the ritual to achieve - and you have to be absolutely clear about this. Even if it is Beltane and you decide you should have a ritual because that's what Pagans do, what is the exact intent?

Above all, it should be remembered that every ritual intends to align the macrocosm and microcosm; to allow the greater forces of the Cosmos to flow through the circle and through the participants, re-forging the links between us and the Gods. Each ritual we perform should progressively make that connection easier and more permanent.

Every act performed in the ritual must be in accord with the intent of the ritual, and this should be reflected in its themes, symbols, words, music and invocations in order to create an harmonic resonance that amplifies that intent. Any false note within any of the above will corrupt the focus of the intent. What happens in the circle has results in the outer world - that's the whole point. Its energies are magnified in the outside world, so that if we introduce anger or chaos, for example, these will be magnified in our lives, the lives of those around us, and the world at large.

THE TIME

After considering the intent of the ritual, you need to decide on when to hold it. Times of year and times of day have distinct energies which will affect the outcome of your ritual. If, for the sake of convenience, you hold your summer solstice ritual on the nearest weekend, you need to be aware that you will be working with a very different energy than if you actually do it on the day. Again, if you do it on the evening of the solstice, this will be very different to doing it at sunrise. The pattern of the phase of the moon, the time of day, the time of year and the alignments of the planets (plus the place and people involved) makes every ritual occasion unique and unrepeatable. The more you can try to make sure these are in harmony with the intent of your ritual, the better.

The time of year (and for us, the Eight Sabbats in particular) marks the relationship between sun and earth. If we identify the Goddess with the earth and the God with the sun, the feminine energy of the Goddess is present throughout the cycle, but the power of the God ebbs and flows throughout the year as the strength of the sun ebbs and flows. In this paradigm, the eight festivals mark his life cycle: he is born at the winter solstice, is nursed at Imbolc, grows to manhood at Ostara, marries the Goddess at Beltane, fertilises her at Midsummer, is honoured as high king at Lughnasa, sacrifices himself for his people at Herfest, rules the land of the dead at Samhain and comes to rebirth at Yule. The festivals mark particular energies entering and leaving our sphere: powers of fertility and increase flood in at Beltane and influences of decay and decline surround us at Samhain. At Beltane we celebrate and harness the energies of growth for the land and for us, personally and spiritually. At Samhain we recognise the inevitability of death; we turn inwards for deep reflection. The magical influences of the two festivals are polar opposites and it should be obvious that you wouldn't work for fertility at Samhain or celebrate a handfasting, despite the fact that I once saw a so-called 'witch' on TV saying it was a good time for love spells! All festivals cannot be celebrated in the same way and the magic is very distinct at each.

In the same way, particular moon phases are used for different rituals. While the moon is a constant presence in the night sky it is ever changing. It has four phases – waxing, full, waning and dark. The waxing (growing) moon is a good time for starting new projects, new relationships and for planting. It is a time for beginnings, things that will grow to fullness in the future. The full moon is used for positive magic- healing, blessing and so on. The energy of the full moon celebrates the fertile, positive, creative forces in the world and in relationships. The waning (shrinking) moon is a time for letting go of bad habits and negative thinking. It is a period of winding down, relinquishing old relationships and situations, purifications and cleansing magic. The days of the dark moon are good for deep inner journeys and meditations, rather than the outward expression of the life-journey. During this dark phase, the moon somehow regenerates itself and begins life anew, just as all life generates in the darkness of the womb or seeds in the dark earth, growing to maturity in the light before ageing and dying and returning to the darkness where life begins again, month after month, season after season, year after year. It should also be remembered that during the course of a month, the moon goes through each of the twelve signs of the zodiac, and this influence can also be employed.

The days of the week, and even the hours of the day, are ruled by the planets. This can become a very complex subject, but in its most basic form:

Sunday - governs employers, friendship, healing and work; it is named after the sun and is sacred to the sun god who rules fertility, passion and sexual energy.
Monday - governs agriculture, psychic ability, witchcraft, the home and medicine; it is named after the moon and is sacred to the moon goddess who rules fertility, feminine power and the emotions.
Tuesday - governs conflict, competition, debates, courage and lust; it is named after the Norse war god Tiw. It is ruled by the planet Mars.
Wednesday – governs study, teaching, divination and communications; it is named after the Germanic chief-god Woden who rules expansive energies, bards and divination. It is ruled by the planet Mercury.
Thursday - governs material things, money, property and luck; it is named after the northern storm god Thor. It is ruled by the planet Jupiter.
Friday - governs love, art, music, incense and perfume making; it is named after Freya or Frigg, the northern goddess of love. It is ruled by the planet Venus.
Saturday - governs the elderly, death, re-incarnation, wills, destruction, death and endings; it is named after the Roman god Saturn and is ruled by the planet Saturn.

THE PLACE

Ideally, every Pagan would like to be work outdoors in some beauty spot, preferably an ancient sacred site. Though this is not usually possible, I would urge you to look for an outdoor location and use it the year round; the longer you work in a particular place, the better the relationship you will build with its energies and spirits, and this will make your rituals far more effective.

Don't expect to simply turn up at a site, demand its energies and clear off afterwards. Before you work anywhere, you must be sure that the spirits of place welcome your attentions and are willing to work with you. You will often sense if you are not welcome, or the spirits may permit you to work there sometimes but not others.

Every place also has its own distinct energies, and you must be sure these are in accord with the intent of your ritual. Don't imagine that every stone circle has healing power, for example: it depends on its alignment and the energies of the land around it. Consider the natural energies of the location in line with the intent of the ritual - a cave would be good for an underworld/womb ritual, a hilltop for midsummer or Lughnasa. You could consider woods, the seashore or secluded parkland, but wherever you hold rituals outside, you need to be sure that it is private - you don't want hikers marching through your circle, or sightseers taking pictures throughout. It is always a good idea to obtain any relevant permissions from the landowners.

I don't really believe in holding rites indoors since Pagan rituals are designed to put us in touch with the forces of Nature, which include wind and rain, but some Pagans make temple rooms in their homes for ritual use. Obviously, unless the owners are rich, such rooms tend to be too small to hold a large number of people, and this limits the size of the magical group. It is important that the temple is only used for ritual and meditation. The living room with the carpet rolled up and the furniture pushed back will never work as well.

Pagan moots and societies often have to meet in a hired hall, hotel or community centre and this is the least favoured option, since there will be restrictions on what you can do. It will also be full of extraneous human energies from its other activities. I'd say avoid it if you can, but if you have no other option, be sure that the proprietors are comfortable with what you are going to do and know what to expect. You will need to do a lot of ritual purification and might have to forgo incense if it is going to set off the fire alarms.

DESIGNING THE RITUAL

Magical traditions have diverse ways of working which emphasise their individual approaches to magic. One way may appeal to Heathens, another to witches or Druids. Even within a single tradition, there are groups that place emphasis on the warrior path, the shamanic path, the bardic path and so on. Whichever it is, any rite will be far more effective if the participants are well schooled in their tradition, and if that tradition is old enough to have opened up its own inner plane contacts. If the rite itself is old and well constructed, it will accrue power over time, more each time it is used. But we all have to start somewhere.

There are a few other things to think about when designing a ritual. Given the intent, the time and the place, you need to consider the type and size of group you are catering for and their level of their training and experience. Coven rituals tend to be more formal with everyone having their own parts to play, but this needs a large degree of training and commitment on the part of the participants. Open rituals might have fewer 'speeches' and include more physical activities such as dancing and music that everyone can join in. (Sadly, many attendees of the latter want something instantly accessible and easily understood without having to put in any thought, effort or work themselves, and are surprised if spiritual fireworks don't result!)

Rituals do not have to be lengthy, complicated or wordy with all the participants learning scripts verbatim. Indeed, if they are, then there is more likelihood that things will go wrong; people will lose concentration or forget what comes next. The most effective rituals are often simple and short. There is a tendency for people to write convoluted rituals that end up with the participants having to read from scripts. I absolutely forbid this in my circles, and there are several reasons for it. Vivianne Crowley wisely points out that while ritual is right brain (the intuitive side) activity; reading is left brain (the logical) side. [e] Reading takes a person out of ritual consciousness and returns them to everyday consciousness. Someone with a script is more intent on finding their place on the page than on the flow of the ritual. Then again, the rustling of bits of paper and the switching on and off of torches make the whole thing farcical.

When I make this point at talks, people often complain that they find it difficult to remember speeches, so they don't. What they really mean is that they can't be bothered to make the effort to spend the weeks coming up to a ritual preparing for it and learning their part. Such laziness is an insult to the Gods. The ancient druids had to learn hundreds of poems and stories, and this mental discipline was an important part of their training for the priesthood. These were the original 'brain-training' exercises, keeping the mind alert, flexible and functioning, and though it is harder to remember things as you get older, this is a good way to combat that deterioration.

On the whole, rather than having written speeches, it is often better that people meditate on the purpose of the ritual and its themes, and when the time comes, speak from the heart in their own words. In fact, is even possible to perform a whole ritual without words, using non-verbal sounds or mime. The performance of the ritual should not become more important than the purpose of the ritual.

A final word - humour has its part to play in ritual, but it should only be used in suitable circumstances e.g. at festivals like Beltane when the Green Man 'threatens' the women with his phallic wand and sexual innuendo flies around the circle. An ill-timed joke can cause the ritual atmosphere to dissipate instantly.

PREPARATION

Preparing for a ritual is not a matter of simply donning your robe and entering the circle. In one sense, the whole of the magician's life is preparation for ritual. He or she learns how to discipline the mind, how to visualise, how to focus on the intent of the rite, how to concentrate for extended periods. He or she studies ritual construction, tables of correspondences, myths and symbolic systems, and works to establish Otherworld contacts.

An essential part of the preparation is the cultivation of a positive state of mind; you must believe that you can and will succeed. Beginners who doubt that rite can accomplish its intent often fail, and blame the ritual or the other members of the group rather than their own lack of abilities or state of preparedness. While a sceptical frame of mind is generally healthy in everyday life and even in your approach to the occult, it should be suspended during a magical operation, as doubt will always cause failure. You have to learn to switch off the rational, questioning part of your mind, what Carlos Castenda called 'the Internal Dialogue', and allow right brain activity to take over. Magic begins in the mind, and the imagination of the magician is the only limiting factor of the magic. Human Will, projected by one who has learned to wield it, potentially has the power of a god.

If you go into the circle thinking about what to make for dinner tomorrow or that you should take the car to the garage to get that odd noise examined, then you won't be able to work effective ritual. If you can't merge into the group mind because you have had an argument with one of the other members and are still feeling resentful, then the intent of the ritual will be warped. You should prepare yourself by removing everyday thoughts, problems, negativity and malice from your mind to make yourself as mentally pure as possible. Meditation is used to clear the mind and focus on the purpose in hand. Coming up to the ritual reflect on your intent. For a seasonal rite, read about the time of year, go for walks and see what is happening in Nature, which is the greatest teacher of all. Study the deeds of the gods and goddesses at this time. Read through the ritual as many times as necessary to fix the order of events in your mind to the point where you do not need to think about them, but can give yourself to its innate flow.

The physical body is prepared with abstinence and fasting to heighten the magician's powers and allow him or her to devote their attention to the forthcoming ceremony. Meat and dairy products are avoided for at least twenty-four hours before the ritual. If you cannot fast during the day of the ritual for medical reasons, eat lightly as a heavy meal will make you more grounded in this reality. Some magicians abstain from sexual activity in the twenty-four hours prior to the ritual to concentrate their life-force. Pagans do not reject the life of the physical body or see it as evil; we are not ascetics. Self-denial is performed for a limited period and for a specific purpose: to heighten the ritual experience.

One of the last stages of preparation is the ritual bath. I use salt and oils of frankincense and rosemary, which cleanse and purify both the body and the aura. Afterwards, I don my ritual garments. I have clothes, robes, cords, jewellery and perfumes that I only wear for ritual and putting these on helps me to focus my mind on what is to come.

If yours is a looser knit group, you should at least let people know that they should prepare themselves mentally and physically for the ritual. However, in an open ritual it is usually necessary to do something on the spot to concentrate the minds of the participants and induce ritual consciousness, though it will never be as effective as the above. Processions to the sacred space can work well, as can dancing, drumming and chanting around the edge of the circle before the ritual begins.

For the ritual itself, make sure that you have everything ready that will be needed in the work ahead: robes, flowers, props and tools etc. Making a check-list is useful.

PREPARATION OF THE RITUAL SPACE

The purpose of setting up a circle aligned to the seven directions (the four quarters, above, below and centre) is to recreate the macrocosm within the microcosm i.e., to create a mirror of the Cosmos within our sacred space. The belief that control of the Cosmos and entry to its various realms can be gained by recreating it in miniature, in a chosen spot, is an ancient one, exemplified by the old Hermetic maxim usually shorted to 'as above, so below'. The creation of stone circles, temples and other sacred sites was an attempt to allow the priest, magician or shaman to manipulate the forces of the macrocosm by recreating it in the microcosm.

According to Plato's *Laws*, the cosmic order is taken as the pattern for any temple or shrine. In the centre stood an *omphalos*, or navel stone, representing the centre of the world. It received the 'world pole' which connected the underworld, earth and heavens. Below the shrine lay the underworld - a sacred well or cave. Around the stone stood shrines to the gods, and the four directions were marked, as well as the twelve winds.

There are too many instances of this recreation of the macrocosm in the microcosm around the world to go into here, but it is found on every continent.

The Sacred Centre

For the ancients creating sacred space, the first thing to determine was the location of the central axis of the country or place. The idea of things having a centre is one that is psychologically important to us and which allows us to orientate ourselves in relationship to it. English villages were once built around a central green and towns around the market cross. The concept that the manifest world has a sacred centre, a foundation point where it connects to the upper and lower world, goes back to at least Neolithic times, and is virtually pan-global:

> *"As the individual's spirit is centralised in the body, and the body has a physical location, so the world's spirit was thought of as centralised at a fixed point."* [f]

Every Celtic country had its own sacred centre. In Ireland it was Tara, situated in the region of Midhe ('Middle'), the royal heart incorporating the *Lia Fail*, the Stone of Density, used for the coronation of the High Kings of Ireland. The kings met there every Beltane at a natural outcrop now known as Aill na Mireann, but probably earlier as *Carraig Choithrigi* ('the Stone of Divisions').

At the centre of our circle, our microcosm, we light the hearth fire. The Neolithic round-house with the fire at the centre in a square hearth, the smoke escaping through the open roof, was also a representation of the Cosmos - the walls of the hut were the circumference of the universe, the hearthstone was the earth, its four sides the four directions and the four seasons. The presence of the gods was manifested in the living fire, with the smoke ascending through the smoke-hole to upperworld of the sky gods.[g] This is reflected in the macrocosm: as the domestic hearth is the sacred centre of the home, the hearth of the gods is the centre of the Cosmos. According to Plato, the twelve Olympian gods (who represent the twelve constellations of the zodiac) circle the House of Heaven, while Hestia the hearth goddess remains still at the centre, tending the hearth, which is called 'the Everlasting Place'.

The Cardinal Points

I suppose it is popularly imagined that the honouring of the four directions was adopted into modern Paganism from Semitic-based ritual magick. However, it has been a tenet of Pagan practice on every continent. Wherever we are is the centre for us. We stand on the earth. Above us are the heavens, the stars turning clockwise about the 'still' Pole Star. Below our feet is the underworld. Beyond this, we generally conceive of directional space as fourfold, what is on our left side, our right side, behind us and before us. The compass reflects this fourfold division, with the cardinal points of the east where the sun rises, the west where it sets, the north where the sun never reaches, and the south, the high point of the sun at noon.

Direction is also important in the Otherworld: when the tribal shaman goes into a trance, he often looks one way and another, the so-called 'quest for the right path' which takes place during rituals.[h] But before we orientate ourselves in the Otherworld, we must first establish our relative place in this and in order to do this properly, the east must be aligned with the true east, the west with the true west and so on. Only then will the microcosm and macrocosm be properly aligned and allow the energies to flow unhindered. The orientation of the circle is not just symbolic.

North:

For Pagans, the north is the sacred direction, the source of great power. For this reason, the altar is set up in the north. Though the casting of the circle begins in the east, the north is acknowledged first.

The north is the cardinal point never touched by the sun, and therefore associated with darkness, midnight, mystery and the unknown. It is the point of the circle allied with the winter solstice, regeneration, rebirth and life through death. In most forms of modern Paganism, the north is associated with the element of earth.

East:

The east is the point of sunrise at the vernal equinox (in case you thought otherwise, the sun doesn't always rise due east), so it is associated with sunrise, Ostara, gestation, growth, illumination and so on. Therefore it was considered a lucky direction, and the Roman legions always marched out to battle through the eastern gate of a city. In most forms of modern Paganism, it is associated with the element of air, breath, inspiration, mind and intellect.

South:

The sun stands highest in the south, so the south is the point of the circle connected with the summer solstice, the zenith of the sun's strength, midday, with things beginning to ripen, maturity and the prime of life, with Will and illumination. Water that runs southward was believed to have powers of healing and counter-magic. The south is usually connected with the element of fire.

West:

The sun sets in the west at the autumn equinox. The west is the place of the dying sun, and is associated with the completion of the harvest, death, age and the unconscious. It is the place of facing our deepest fears. The west is also connected to water, creativity and the emotions.

In European mythology, the entrance to the Otherworld is in the west, often through bodies of water where the sun seems to sink into them. Legendary fairy isles - such as Avalon- where the apple trees bear fruit and blossom together, always lie in the west. Neolithic and Bronze Age paradises were orchards - indeed 'paradise' means 'orchard'. The round, red apple is a symbol of the sun or sun god who dies each night to enter the Land of Youth, travelling through the realms of the dead to the east and rebirth with each dawn. In ancient Egyptian lore, the sun god 'died' in the west each night and travelled through the underworld to be reborn at dawn in the east. The dead were said to travel with him. Some Irish houses still have a *seomra thiar* ("western room"), an alcove dedicated to the family dead, containing souvenirs and photographs.[i]

North - EARTH
EAST - AIR
SOUTH - FIRE
WEST - WATER

In ancient cities, there were often four gates at the four cardinal directions. The western gate was considered unlucky, corresponding as it does to the place of the dying sun. This was certainly true in Minoan and Roman lore. Roman messengers bearing bad news entered by this gate; the dead were carried out of it and men condemned to execution were taken out of the city via it. Troops on their way to battle would never leave by the western gate. At first and second degree initiation, the candidate enters through the western gate, the gate of death, having spent time in the western realm of the dead.

FINISHING TOUCHES

Once the circle has been set up and properly aligned, you can create the right environment with incense, oils, decorations and coloured candles etc. but they should be chosen with care to reflect the intent of the ritual. Before the rite commences, everything must be in a state of readiness. Anything needed for the rite should be at hand and in its proper place. Anything which should not be in the circle must be removed. Some witches sweep the circle with the besom as a final act of purification.

THE RITUAL PROPER:

THE SPIRITS OF PLACE ARE INVITED AND HONOURED

To begin, we honour the spirits of fur and feather, of rock and crystal, of tree and herb as well as the spirits of the Ward that protect the land, and the indwelling spirits of place. We invite them to come to our circle and join in our celebrations. We ask them to welcome us and work with us to achieve our purpose in fellowship and mutual respect. If we feel that they do not want us to be there we will pack up and go home as it would be foolish and even dangerous to continue.

THE COSMIC AXIS IS CONNECTED

There are similarities in Pagan beliefs across the world, even though many of these societies never had any contact: all believe in a tiered Cosmos, usually of three realms –upper world, middle world and lower world. The ancient Babylonians spoke of the heavenly realm of Shamash (the sun god), the middle world of humans and the underworld of the dead. Even the Christian world-view sees man in the centre, with heaven above and hell below.

Middle Earth or the middle realm is the everyday world where we live, the place of mundane life and ordinary consciousness, the place of revealed creation. It is situated between the realms of above and below. Spirits from the other realms may break through into the everyday world, sometimes in the form of omens and other signs.

The underworld exists 'below' us. It is the primeval darkness, the realm of the dead and the unborn, a sometimes frightening and wild place where dreams and nightmares take on substance. It is called the womb of the Goddess where life begins and where the dead lie. It is the realm of the ancestors and the land of the sidhe. The underworld is reached (in vision) through caves, wells, by sinking or diving under the sea or rivers, by climbing down a hollow tree into its roots, or through the tomb.

Traditionally, the Upperworld ranges from the sky to the heavens, and contains the higher planes of existence, the realm of the sky gods. It is usually reached by climbing the World Tree or pole, or perhaps by flying on the back of a bird, in the form of a bird, or by crossing the Rainbow Bridge.

The realms are connected by the World Tree or central pole, the cosmic axis which stood at the centre of the world, or the centre of the kingdom. Often, these were physically represented with a pole, pillar or tree. This cosmic axis was considered the legitimate source of human law and was represented by the measuring rod, the king-post and the sceptre.[j] Every Celtic chief had a measuring rod which he received at his installation. By virtue of this rod he was able to mete out justice, as well as measure the kingdom to find its centre.

Another representation of the cosmic axis is the World Tree, with its roots in the netherworld, trunk in middle earth, and branches in the heavens. The most famous example is the Norse Yggdrasil, an evergreen ash tended by the Norns, three goddesses of fate who live at its roots, moistening them with water from the Well of Urdur.

In Judaic and Christian myth, the tree of knowledge grew in Paradise ('orchard'), but the first man and woman, Adam and Eve, were forbidden to pluck its fruits. Tempted by the serpent at its roots, Eve plucked the fruit of knowledge and gave it to Adam. God grew angry at this trespass, and flung them from Paradise. Eve's original Hebrew name was Hawwah from the Akkadian word *Hayah* meaning 'to live'. She is thus called Hawwah because she was 'Mother of All Living' according to Genesis. This was a title of the Sumerian goddess Ninhursag from whom the myth was appropriated by the Hebrews. In the Sumerian version the god Enki (possibly cognate with Yahweh or Jehovah) was cursed by Ninhursag because he stole forbidden plants from paradise. His health began to fail and the other gods prevailed on the Mother Goddess to help him. She created a goddess called Ninti (literally *nin*= lady, *ti*= rib i.e. 'lady of the rib', a play on words since the phrase also means 'to make live'). Enki claimed his rib hurt him and she healed him. Eve is in fact the Great Goddess, who initiates Adam into her mysteries via the World Tree.

The Cosmos is conceived of as spinning around this central pole, which remains still. The sense of the world spinning about the still cosmic axis is reflected in the image of spinning wool about a distaff. Our Anglo-Saxon and Scandinavian ancestors believed that the goddess Freyja span out the web of destiny. In Norse tradition, the three stars we know as the belt of Orion are called 'Freyja's Distaff', or perhaps they represent the three Norns spinning each person's wryd (fate). [k] There are many other ancient spinning and weaving goddesses who spin the thread of the Cosmos and weave the web of destiny, such as the Greek Fates.

The revolution of the stars around the apparently still Pole Star near the centre of the heavens could readily be taken to mean that the polar region of the stars was the centre of the Cosmos. It was the point in the heavens where the central pole connected. It was called the *Nowl* in Norse lore, which means 'navel' or the 'nail' which holds the sky in position. In Celtic tradition, the Spiral Castle of Arianrhod (the Corona Borealis) surrounds the North Star, and this is the place that souls travel to at death or for initiation.

For these reasons, at the beginning of ritual, the cosmic axis is drawn through the centre of the ring, from the heavens above, through the hearth-fire and down into the underworld. Thus we are linked to all three realms so that we are truly 'between the worlds'.

THE RING IS DRAWN

The next act is to define the ritual area by drawing a circle around the boundaries of the ring. Wiccans do this with the steel athame or sword, but in Wicce we admit no iron or steel to our ring (because spirits are deterred by such metal), and do this with a bronze or silver knife or on some occasions with the wand or hand alone. This marks it out as consecrated space, a place where gods and humans can communicate, where the mundane meets the sacred.

The circle is a universal symbol of wholeness and completion. The whole circle symbolises continuity, eternity, completion and spacelessness: the absence of time and space. As it symbolises what is complete and unbroken, it also symbolises Deity and everlasting love.

But the circle can be divided: halved, quartered or separated into degrees and so on. However, far from symbolising dissolution and imperfection, when these fractions are contained within the circle they represent the balance and harmony of such divisions. Within the circle, opposites (such as day and night, summer and winter) are united. Within the circle their division is not absolute, but each gives rise to the other, reconciled in the circle of unity.

Ritual magicians treat the circle as a barrier that protects them from the sometimes dangerous powers they invoke. I often read that modern Wiccans use the circle to contain the power they raise. In the Traditional Craft, the ring is neither of those things. It is an interface between the worlds, between the physical realm and the Otherworld.

THE GATES ARE OPENED

In turn, the priest or priestess opens the gateways to the powers of the east, south, west and north, the elemental kingdoms. Again, this is different from ritual magic and modern Wicca, when the Guardians of the Watchtowers are summoned by command to the circle, and bidden to watch and guard it. We ask them to open the gateways to their realms, so that the elemental powers may flow into the ring along the four Royal Roads to meet at the centre of the circle, where all times and all places are one, and all are accessible. The Otherworld is around us, eternal, timeless, where Nature and human consciousness know no separation. It does not exist in some distant place, and space is only a metaphor for expressing our separation from it. It is here, not there. [1] By his actions, the magician reunites the worlds.

Airy spirits of the winds
Gentle breath of the dawn
Arise and come unto me this night.

Burning spirits of the flame
Transforming as you devour
Arise and come unto me this night.

Misty spirits of the waters
Haunters of the twilight pools
Arise and come unto me this night.

Elementals of the rich, moist soil
Earth-spirits of rock, stone and crystal
Arise and come unto me this night.

THE PARTICIPANTS ARE ADMITTED

The circle can be cast with all the participants inside, or it may be cast by the Fetch/ Weaver and priest/ess with the rest of the coven outside. If the latter is the case, this is the point where the rest of the participants are admitted, stepping across the threshold which separates the world of men from the place of mysteries. The threshold may be formed by the besom, or crossed besom and sword (in those traditions which admit iron). This is spoken of as 'passing the gate'. Most covens ask for a password at the point, and it is no secret than many use the phrase 'Perfect Love and Perfect Trust' which is a useful reminder to the group that such is the state in which they must approach the mysteries.

THE GODS ARE INVOKED

The next stage of the ritual is to invoke the gods themselves. A true ritual is more than a performance that mentally stimulates the participants with theatre; it opens a channel to the higher powers:

> "*...it is not enough to cry Lord, Lord, loudly and persistently; there must be an adequate equipment of scholarship and organization of the physical plane to enable the spiritual forces to find a channel.*" Dion Fortune

At first, until a group has opened up higher plane channels of their own, they may simply address the God and Goddess and invite them to be present for the duration of the ritual. However, when the priest or priestess is sufficiently advanced, the God and Goddess are invoked, called into the circle or into the bodies of the presiding priest and priestess. There is a difference between invocation and evocation that is sometimes confused; indeed, both words have several possible interpretations:

Invocation:

1. To call a spirit or a deity into the circle.
2. To invite possession by a spirit or deity.

Evocation:

1. Evoke means 'to call up or produce'. For a ceremonial magician (i.e. a non-Pagan magician working in the Cabalistic, Hermetic etc. tradition), it means to call forth a physical manifestation of a spirit or deity onto the astral or physical plane, usually outside the circle in the triangle of art, or into a crystal or black mirror. The adept is then thought to be able to bind the entity to his will.

2. In psychodrama, the gods are seen merely as fragmented parts of the human personality and not outside forces at all. In this case, ritual becomes a method of integrating the fragments into the whole.

3. In Paganism, evocation is often used to mean to call forth an echo of a spirit or deity from within. This is used when a person personates a god within the circle. To find a connection with the god, he calls forth from within the part of himself that corresponds with the god. In a purely psychological sense, it evokes the part of the self represented by the god, or goddess, as love is represented by Venus, compassion by Demeter, aggression by Ares and so on. Moreover, when a god is invoked into the body of a priest or priestess, invocation and evocation are both used. It is said that when a deity is invoked, it evokes an echo of the same vibration

within the self, which responds and connects. It is a brief melding, but one which has a permanent effect on the priest or priestess.

When the initiate invokes possession by a god, he opens himself to the energies he calls upon, allowing the Cosmic forces (the specified god or goddess) to flood his soul with the forces of life, bridging the gap between himself and the Gods. In order to do this, he evokes the corresponding spark within himself of that essence. If we remember that the microcosm (us) is a mirror of the macrocosm (the Cosmos) everything that is contained within the Cosmos also exists within us. That means there is an echo of every kind of god-energy within each of us:

"The principle of universal order is that in one is all, and this naturally includes the spiritual innateness of the material world. Body, mind, spirit, fetch and soul are one with the Cosmos. No part of it is unworthy, for there is no part of us that is not of the divine and no part of the divine that is not within material existence."[m]

In order to do this, the magician has to train himself to be an empty and suitable vessel for the god-energy. He must have meditated on that god-essence, his symbols and mythologies, and be able to visualise the god-form easily and precisely. While concentrating on the form of the god, he calls upon the name of the god as many times as are needed, the vibration of the name awakening in him an echo of the macrocosmic power. He feels that form surrounding him, and the form becoming his own. Sometimes the observer will note a change in the features of the priest and he may seem to get taller, shorter, thinner or stockier. The priest will feel flooded with dynamic energy and intense emotions.

Just because the gods are called, it does not always mean that they will answer. You need to know what exactly you have contacted and invoked. It helps if you know how to correctly pronounce the names of the deities you are invoking. My name is Anna, but I often get called Ann or Hannah. I don't answer to either simply because I don't realise it is me that is being addressed.

Unless the acting priest or priestess has an open channel to that deity, established through custom, then the god will not answer the call. Often it will take many unsatisfactory and fruitless rituals before contact is established and the presence of the deity felt. Patience is a necessary virtue for the ritualist and those people who want fast results for little effort will be sadly disillusioned. It takes time to establish a contact with a deity, to raise consciousness to the level where it can be aware of the true essence of the being's nature. The Gods are always there, not subject to the same temporal considerations that we are, but we need to be in a certain state of mind in order to perceive them. When you understand the essence of an entity and accept it into your world view, your essence and its essence can merge, and you can become that being for a time; any separation between you vanishes.

When taking on a god form, it is necessary to find an echo of that god's power within the self, searching deep into the unconscious mind for the corresponding energies. If you do not know yourself well, including your weaknesses and vices, you may be in jeopardy. There are entities out there which will be attracted to your shadow side, and are alerted to your presence when you dabble in magical ritual without proper precautions. When that entity is stronger than you - and it probably is - your will becomes subsumed it its will. Unwary and untrained magicians have lost their minds entirely in the process.

Some occultists claim that the Gods and spirits are but fragmented parts of the human consciousness or the archetypal products of mankind's imagination over centuries, aspects of the psyche that need to be acknowledged and tamed. Probably in ninety per cent of cases this is the true nature of the supposed deities and spirits contacted by would-be ritualists. Nonetheless, as Pagans, we know the Gods are real, as is our ability to contact them, however often we fail. We acknowledge that they have a separate existence, intelligence and awareness, not to mention their own paths and purposes; they are not there to serve our whims. Cosmic forces are not to be contacted lightly or randomly. We should approach them only when fully prepared, respectfully; using ritual to control and regulate the exchange.

OFFERING

Before we can receive, we must first give - and this is the old law. We begin by making an offering of incense to the spirits and Gods before we go any further. Later on, we will make another offering of bread and wine. At different times of year, we may make other gifts to the Gods, such as songs and poetry and seasonal food. We do not make any gifts that bring about suffering and death, so animals foods and sacrifices are never employed, but simply flowers, foods and decorations; things that will biodegrade or that can be eaten by the animals of the woodlands. The only exception to this is the offering of the blood of the Sacred King at Herfest, who chooses to make sacrifice to the Earth Mother for the good of the land and clan. Sacrifice comes from the Latin and means 'to make sacred'.

STATEMENT OF INTENT

The magical dictum is 'intention is everything'. A ritual is never performed for its own sake, for the sake of its poetry or beauty, but always has a specific purpose. If the rite has no purpose, there should be no rite. You have to be very clear what the intention of the ritual is and express it unambiguously. You have to let the people and spirits invited to the ritual know what they are being invited to, what the event is for. Anything open to misinterpretation will be misinterpreted. Magic, like water, always seeks the easiest course to the sea.

During ritual the intent, which first exists in the group mind, is created on the astral and then channelled into the physical realm using the power raised by the ritual. When a group frequently works together, a group mind is fashioned from all the participants concentrating together on the same object. The power of a group of people concentrating on a single object is considerable. They are lifted together out of mundane consciousness and become more than human for a moment in time, changing consciousness together to the level required by the ritual. When all focus on a natural force, that force will find a channel of manifestation through the form thus built up on the astral, and the celebrants will feel an inrush of the power that has been invoked. When this is frequently repeated, that image remains on the astral and the force is permanently concentrated. According to the occult law of contact, connections once established continue to interact long after separation (just as subatomic particles that have been in contact continue to influence each other long after they have been moved apart) [n]: after all, we are all part of the One.

POWER IS RAISED

The traditional way of raising power for ritual is by using dance. When you move with conscious intent and purpose, the power released can be immense. As in other areas of magic, you need to lose your ego and move in concert with the rhythm of the ritual. It won't work if you are conscious of feeling silly or worrying about the steps; only when the steps are mastered can the dancer surrender to the dance and become one with the pattern of the dance, experiencing its transformative energies. We dance and are danced, and find ourselves engaged in a great mysterious conversation:

> *"We're really praying" Drissana Devananda, a Tantric dancer, said. "It's a devotional practice. We're not bodies seeking the spirit, but spirits seeking bodily experience. Dance is about remembering to function from our whole bodies, the "body mind". That is the place we remember the Goddess."*[o]

It is said that dance is the original form of sacred worship. Every part of the world uses dance as a means of expression, celebration and marking the passing seasons. Dances were used to plead with the gods for rain, for sunshine, to provide good harvests. It was used to mark births, marriages and deaths, the coming of age. The role of sacred dance is most often seen among goddess worshipping cultures where priestesses and priests utilised it as part of ritual and healing. Indeed, dance was one of the primary forms of expressing goddess worship and the goddess was often portrayed as a dancer who danced the pattern of the seasons and the cycles of being.

When everyone takes hands it represents the completion of the circle, the symbol of oneness and harmony. In the circle we hold hands with one palm up and the other down. This allows the energy to flow right round the circle from person to person. Everyone is connected with each other, with the dance and with the circle. This creates a feeling of harmony and connection among the group that often results in a feeling of connection with the Gods. In such a dance all are equal; there is no leader and no follower, all moving together but expressing individual feelings. This is one of the devices used to bring about a cohesion and unity in the ritual, where people move together in spirit, towards a common purpose. It doesn't matter whether everybody moves in exactly the same way, but the movement in the same direction is important.

Another way of raising power is through the use of chants. Some Craft chants are meaningless words, repeated for the trance inducing sounds of the syllables. Others focus the mind on a specific idea. Chants and drumming are useful for inducing the light trance needed for ritual consciousness. It is the persistent, monotonous nature of the beat which makes this possible. All religions use chants and liturgies to affect the consciousness of the congregations. The most effective chants are repetitive and quite monotonous. Chanting obviously affects the breathing, in a similar manner to yogic breathing. Breathing is an important discipline, and learning to slow your breathing will help you relax. Part of the initiate's training includes performing regular breathing exercises. This will also help with the projection of the voice during ritual, which should be pitched so that the other celbrants can hear clearly, and should not consist of an apologetic mumble which will impress neither man nor spirit. The words of the song or chant should emphasize the purpose, and relate to the practitioner's symbolic system to reinforce the power. By moving and chanting together, an attuned group can enter a new realm of consciousness as a group mind and work together within the magical reality.

THE BODY OF THE RITUAL IS PERFORMED

The performance of a ritual brings it to life, bridging the gap between us and the Gods. Speaking its words fills them with power.

The theme of the ritual needs to fit the occasion and its intent. The more cohesive the theme and its expression, the more successful the ritual will be in achieving its intentions. What is the general feel of the occasion? Is it joyful and playful as it might be at Beltane, or solemn and grave, as it might be at Samhain? Which set of mythologies are you working with, which pantheon? Never, ever mix traditions, cultures and pantheons as only chaos can result. Working with the Gods and spirits of the land you stand on is always more powerful than calling in foreign deities, unless you are strongly connected to them by blood and culture.

During the ritual, the movements of the celebrants may try to echo the movements of the Gods, planets or cosmic patterns to reproduce in microcosm what is happening (or desired) in macrocosm. This communicates to the participants without words, on a direct and fundamental level.

To enact a ritual drama, one or more of the celebrants might wear the mask or clothing of a deity, just as the ancient Egyptian priests wore the masks of their gods. For instance, at Yule one of the men of our coven stands for the new-born Sun God, and is armed to conquer the dark by visiting each of the quarters and being given sword, crown, sash and staff. In this case, a priest will try to identify with the god and his myth:

> *"In traditional cultures, masks, drama and dance are about contacting the divine, and refreshing the mythologies that inform their cultures."* [p]

In such cultures, masks are made with the aim of embodying spirit within them, by making them with the right materials, in the right circumstances with the right intent and proper consecration. When a man or woman wears the mask, he or she animates that spirit. As long as the mask remains in use it is considered to contain spirit and between ceremonies it is treated with respect and even given offerings. When a mask is de-animated and laid to rest, this is done with ceremony and due honour. [q]

Every part of the ritual should flow naturally to the next without any awkward pauses and loss of focus. Establishing sufficient group focus to do this necessitates the use of visual, emotional, and sensory keys. Every object in the ritual should be evocative of the theme expressed by the ceremony. Everything that can heighten the concentration and emotion is employed: a powerful ritual engages all the senses. Gesture, symbol and visual stimuli are very important. Flickering flames add to the atmosphere, as do the robes, headdresses and masks of the celebrants, with their meaningful colours and designs. Every word spoken in the ritual must act on the sense of hearing to focus the mind on the ritual intent. Chants and mantras can have a powerful effect on the mind, as can certain notes and frequencies. Perfumes and incenses are used to evoke certain sensations. The sense of taste is addressed with the cakes and wine. The sense of touch is used throughout; when you take the hands of your companions: you should be aware of what it is you are sharing.

Rituals, by their very nature, are often experimental- we try to find out what works, what techniques get us the results we want. Rituals are not written in stone, or at least, they should not be. There should be room for evolution and growth but this doesn't mean changing things for the sake of change- if something works, stick with it, but be aware that there may be ways to make it better.

After the body of the ritual, we perform any magic such as healing that is required. Then there is always a quiet period of meditation to allow space for the Gods to speak directly to the celebrants, or manifest in the form of omens.

RITUAL CONSUMPTION OF BREAD AND WINE

The dedication of the bread and wine is one of the central points of every Pagan ritual. Eating bread and drinking wine was an important part of the rites of harvest goddesses and vegetation gods throughout the world, and pre-dates Christianity by millennia.

Foods have always played an key part in rituals and the worship of the Gods. Without food we would not live at all, and its production was one of the central themes of ancient religions. Mysteriously, the small seed planted beneath the dark earth would shoot and grow into something that would provide a sustaining meal. It was as though by placing it in the womb of Mother Earth she would nourish and sustain it, magically transforming it just as a woman would nurture the seed in her womb to produce a child.

Catholics believe that the bread and wine is the transubstantiated flesh and blood of God: in other words, the bread and wine become the flesh and blood of God with the act of consecration. For ancient Pagans, grain and wine were god-essences intrinsically. When we consecrate bread and wine in a ritual, we invoke this god-essence, the spiritual core of the food; through it, we absorb the power of the Gods. When we eat the bread, we take in the life-force of the Corn God and it nourishes us, physically and spiritually.[r]

Wine is one of the 'god-containing' substances believed by the ancients to allow people to share in God-consciousness. Whereas bread is viewed as the body of the sacrificed god, wine is his blood, or sometimes it is seen as the blood of the Earth Goddess. In our tradition, the bread reflects the God and the wine the Goddess: the masculine and the feminine; the earth and the heavens; the solid and the liquid - the taking of the two together signifies the union of opposites. The cup that contains the wine symbolises the cauldron or grail, which contains wisdom and inspiration.

The chalice of wine and the platter of bread are passed around the circle with the words "Blessed Be" to be shared by all present with love and blessings. This intimate act creates a connection with every other person present as well as a communion with the Gods. It comes at the end of the ritual and helps to ground the participants before the circle is broken.

Bread

Bread is called 'the staff of life' and came to ritually symbolise all other food. One of the most valuable of the ancient foods was grain, which could be made into flour and then bread. It is one of the most important symbols of the nurturing Goddess. It was often seen as her son, a god in itself, given life by the spirit of the Corn Lord who would awaken in the spring, grow through the summer and mature in the autumn, only to be harvested and die. The shed seeds lay dormant in the cold, winter earth, the belly of the Earth Mother, ready to shoot again in the spring. This was a never ending cycle of life, death and rebirth, a cycle also promised to worshippers. This story was recalled in songs among farming folk until recent times:

There were three men came out of the West
Their fortunes for to find,
And these three men made a solemn vow,
'John Barleycorn must die'.
They've ploughed, they've sown, they've harrowed him in
Through plods of barley's head,
And these three men made a solemn vow,
'John Barleycorn is dead'.
They let him lie for a very long time,
'Til the rains from heaven did fall,
And little Sir John sprung up his head
And so amazed them all.
They've let him stand until Mid-Summer's Day
'Til he looked both pale and wan,
And little Sir John's grown a long, long beard
And so become a man.

They've hired men with the scythes so sharp
To cut him off at the knee,
They've rolled him and tied him by the way
Serving him most barbarously.

They've hired men with the sharpest hooks
Who've pricked him to the heart,
And the Loader, he has served him worse than that,
For he's bound him to the cart.

They've wheeled him around and around a field
'Til they came unto a barn,
And there they made a solemn oath
On poor John Barleycorn.

They've hired men with the crofting sticks
To cut him skin from bone,
And the Miller, he has served him worse than that,
For he's ground him between two stones.

And little Sir John and the nut brown bowl,
And he's brandy in the glass,
And little Sir John and the nut brown bowl
Proved the strongest man at last.

The huntsman he got off the fox
Oh so loudly to blow his horn,
And the tinker he can't mend kettle nor pots
Without a little Barleycorn.

The narrative is clear- John Barleycorn, the spirit of the corn, is cut down and buried in the earth, seeming to be dead, but when the spring rains come he is resurrected and grows with the summer sun. With the late summer he begins to wither and weaken, and his head droops. He ages as autumn comes and his enemies cut him down. They tie him up on a cart (the sheaves of corn are gathered, tied and carted away), they beat him up (flail the grain), wash him, toss him about (winnow the grain), roast the marrow from his bones (scorch the grain) and grind him between two stones (mill the grain), then drink his blood (the alcohol brewed from the barley).

This echoes the story of the Egyptian Osiris imprisoned in a coffin (buried), dismembered and scattered (the corn is winnowed and the seeds scattered) and resurrected (the seed-corn grows in the spring). The followers of Osiris ate wheat cakes, marked with a cross, which embodied the god.

In Greece and the near East, Adonis, Tammuz and Dumuzi are also torn apart, forced to go into the underworld and are resurrected in the spring. The death and rebirth of the goddess Cybele's lover Attis was celebrated at the spring equinox, first with a day of blood on Black Friday and culminated after three days in a day of rejoicing over his resurrection. Sound familiar? It gets more so. Attis was born of a human woman, a virgin named Nana on 25th December. He was known as a saviour of humankind by way of his sacrificial death, crucified on a pine tree so that his holy blood could pour down to redeem the earth.

Vegetation gods were often given the title 'saviour' because they give their lives so that mankind might live, often spoken of as incarnated gods, like Osiris and Dionysus. This poem by Euripes was written 480 or 485–406 BCE:

Behold, God's Son is come unto this land
Of heaven's hot splendour lit to life, when she
Of Thebes, even I, Dionysus, whom the brand
Who bore me, Cadmus' daughter Semele
Died here. So, changed in shape from god to man,

I walk again by Dirce's streams and scan
Ismenus' shore.[s]

The flesh of the gods was eaten in the form of wheaten cakes. For a thousand years before Christianity, Mithras was worshipped widely among the Persians, Indians, Romans and Greeks, up till around 400 CE. Mithras was born in a cave of a virgin mother, attended by shepherds, on December 25th and his religion spread with the Roman Empire and nearly took over the known world. He was the known as the 'Light of the World', 'The Redeemer' and 'The Good Shepherd'. He baptised his followers and shared a Last Supper. An inscription on the temple of Mithras which lies beneath the Vatican reads: *"He who will not eat of my body, nor drink of my blood, so that he may be one with me and I with him, shall not be saved,"* a saying later attributed to Jesus. He travelled far and wide as a teacher and had twelve companions. He was buried in a tomb and rose again at the spring equinox, which was celebrated with great rejoicing.

In Mexico, the god Xiuhzilopoctli was commemorated in the festival of 'eating the god' when people ate a dough image of the god raised on a cross.

When vegetation gods die they are said to go into the underworld (the seed is planted beneath the earth). Here they often become kings of the underworld and the dead- Crom Dubh was underworld ruler of the mounds, Osiris was Lord of the Dead, Dumuzi was Lord of the Abyss, Adonis became the lover of the Queen of the Underworld and so on.

An ear of corn was the central mystery of the worship of Demeter at Eleusis. Bread was eaten at the rites of Artemis and Cybele and other earth and moon goddesses, often baked in circles and marked with a cross, representing the four directions, the four phases of the moon and the four solar festivals. This is still seen today in our hot crossed buns eaten at Easter, which was once the springtime celebration of the resurrection of the vegetation god, as well as the Christian's communion wafers.

The bread is sometimes dipped in salt, which preserves foods and makes them incorruptible, representing permanence and immortality. It also symbolises wisdom and truth, and was formerly used in funeral rites to keep the soul safe from evil spirits. For the same reason it was placed on the tongues of newly born children. Bread and salt represented hospitality and to share them imposed obligations on both the giver and receiver, the sacred duties of host and guest.

Festival bread is made especially for the ritual. It is made with due ceremony and intent; buying a machine-made loaf from the supermarket just isn't good enough as an offering to the Gods. In many parts of the world, different breads are made for different occasions, their shapes and varieties reflecting the festival and its symbolism. Traditional loaf-shapes are based upon binding knots or in the shape of suns and moons, animals and humans. [t] It would be appropriate to have a sun-shaped loaf for Midsummer, or one in the form of a sheaf of wheat for Lughnasa, and so on.

In many books on witchcraft cakes, rather than bread, are described as being used in the consecration ceremony. According to Leland's *Aradia*, these were traditionally made from meal, salt, honey and wine and shaped as crescent moons.[u] We generally used bread in loaves suitable shaped for the season, but you could use crescent moon shaped scones.

The bread is put to bake with a blessing, such as:

"Let the bread be baked in the name of ...(the Goddess) for now is the time of the... feast, when the secret worshippers meet once more. Before the Goddess we shall drain the cup. Before the Goddess we shall serve the secret rites. Before the Goddess we shall feast and rejoice. In the holy name of...(the God) and in the holy name of...(the Goddess)"

Wine

Notice that the alcohol brewed from John Barleycorn is called his blood. There are two gifts of the vegetation god - bread from his body, and wine (or beer) from his blood.

The ancients thought that the state induced by wine was a sacred one, a communion with the mind of the God. The term 'entheogen' was invented by Gordon Wasson, and means 'god containing' and refers to plants that have the ability to allow people to unite with god-consciousness. All plants which had the ability to change consciousness were considered sacred or god-containing, but wine is more palatable than most, added to the fact that the vine grows in a spiral pattern, a very ancient symbol of immortality. Wine was thought not to feed the body but the spirit, conferring the divine inspiration of the God, freeing the imbiber from logical thoughts and moral conventions, awakening the powers of the primal, instinctive self within.

The story of the wine god is seen most clearly in the myth of Dionysus (Bacchus). He was the son of Zeus and Semele, a mortal woman. Whilst pregnant, Semele asked to see Zeus in his true form. He warned her that her human frame could not withstand his glory and tried to refuse. Undaunted, she insisted and forced him to agree. The god had spoken the truth, and the power that radiated from him destroyed Semele. To save his unborn son, Zeus took the foetus from her womb and incubated it in his thigh so instead of being born in the usual way, Dionysus sprang from his father's body fully formed, on December 25th, at once both god and human. The followers of Dionysus celebrated his 'advent' with a newborn baby placed in a winnowing basket – the forerunner of baby Jesus in the manger.

Zeus knew that his jealous wife Hera would try to harm the child and smuggled him away to be brought up by foster parents who disguised the young demi-god as a girl. However, Hera was not easily fooled and began her revenge by driving the foster parents mad. Zeus then turned Dionysus into a goat kid and sent him to be cared for by the nymphs of Mount Nysa. This proved equally unsafe as the Titans enticed him away from his guardians, tore him into pieces and boiled him up in a cauldron. Once again, Zeus intervened to save his son. At his behest, the goddess Athene saved his heart while Zeus rescued his limbs. Apollo buried them on the slopes of Mount Parnassus where the goddess Rhea brought them back to life.

When Dionysus grew up he discovered the culture of the vine and the method of making wine, but Hera struck him with madness, and drove him forth a wanderer across the face of the earth. In Phrygia the goddess Cybele (or Rhea to the Greeks), cured him and taught him her religious rites, and he set out on a progress through Asia teaching the people the cultivation of the vine. Dionysus' madness may be considered in the light of a shamanic crisis. Indeed, one of his powers was communication between the living and the dead. His spring festival, the Anthesteria, the festival of the vine flower, was also a feast of the dead when souls were believed to walk the streets again. The god was celebrated as having returned from the realm of the dead, but it was recognised that life and death are insolubly connected.

Dionysus is known as Lyaeus ('he who unties'), a god who frees his followers from the constraints of everyday life and its worries:

Possessed, ecstatic, he leads their happy cries;
the earth flows with milk, flows with wine,
flows with the nectar of bees;
The air is thick with a scent of Syrian myrrh.
The celebrant runs entranced, whirling the torch
That blazes red from the fennel-wand in his grasp,
And with shouts he rouses the scattered bands,
Sets their feet dancing,
As he shakes his delicate locks to the wild wind. [v]

The Greater Dionysia was celebrated at the spring equinox, when vegetation is renewed and the god danced down the hills calling upon women to leave their chores and join his wild celebrations and experience his religious ecstasy.

In December the Lesser Dionysia was celebrated, when Dionysus rose from the dead at Delphi, and ruled the three months of winter while Apollo, the sun god, was away. Dionysus was called *Melanaigis* ('he with the black goat-skin') and a combat between 'the Light One' and 'the Black One' was enacted. Dionysus was a god that defied the social order, broke taboos and customs and gained knowledge through divine madness, attracted to the night and dark places. As such he was the opposite of the god Apollo, logical, dignified, lord of the sun and daylight. They perhaps represent the two sides of human consciousness, both necessary in balance. They were often seen as representing the two halves of the year, Apollo the light and Dionysus the dark.

Around the world, alcohol has been, and in most places is still used at times of celebration and to honour the Gods. In Germanic cultures, the sacred mead-horn was passed among the participants in rituals and ceremonies. Elsewhere, special brews were made to reflect the time of year and the drinking of the new wine was a great occasion. Even today, breweries make special beers to mark great occasions.[w]

Country wines can be made with seasonal ingredients – strawberries at midsummer, blackberries at Herfest, hawthorn flowers at Beltane and so on. Our favourite for Samhain is sloe gin and for Yule we always have mead.

The wine should preferably be home made and put to brew with a blessing such as:

> *"Let the wine be made ready in the name of …(the God) and in the name of …(the Goddess). Let it be placed on the altar beneath the sign of the pentagram that the worshippers shall drink of it. Before the God and the Goddess we shall consume and be consumed by the wine of wisdom and blessing. Before the Lord and Lady we shall consume the cakes and wine. Before …(the God) and …(the Goddess)."*

The Blessing of the Cakes and Wine

This is done in different ways by different Pagan groups and traditions. In some covens, the consecration is done by a priest and priestess together. The priestess might hold the cup while the priest plunges his athame into it and one of them will speak the blessing. In those groups that believe polarity is reversed on the astral, the priest holding the cup (the feminine) and the priestess plunges her knife (the masculine) into it and utters the words of consecration. In other groups, the priestess will bless the wine and the priest the bread, or vice versa. We like to share this task out between coven members so that at each festival a different person is responsible for blessing both the cakes and wine. (The only occasion where this is not pre-decided is at Lughnasa, where the God-chosen new king performs the act). They are asked to write their own words for this, which makes them consider what the ceremony means.

There are many blessings outlined in various books and websites, and here are just a few:

> *"I conjure thee O wine, the light of the sun and the light of the moon have ripened the swelling grape- the blood of the earth pressed smooth. I conjure thee, O wine, that as we drink of thee, we drink of the power of the God: the fire and lightening and rain; the things that are wild and free."*

"I conjure thee O meal, who art indeed our body, since without thee we would not live. Thou, who art at first a seed, before becoming flour. I conjure thee, O meal, that when we partake of thee, we partake of the wisdom of the Goddess: we learn more of the fields and the forests; we see more of the ancient ways and know the ancient laws."

An Alexandrian Wiccan blessing of wine:

As the athame is to the male, so the chalice is to the female; and conjoined, they are one in blessedness.

O Queen, most secret, bless this food unto our bodies; bestowing health, wealth, strength, joy and peace, and that fulfilment of love which is perfect happiness.

This is one I wrote for the Mercian Gathering, held during harvest time, which shows that the consecration can be adapted to suit the time of year:

Priest: I eat, yet it is not bread I eat but the body of the God, sprung from the womb of the Earth, ripening under the sun. I eat and salute the sun, praying to the God that he will guard the corn until the harvest is complete and his sacrifice made. May the crops be good!

Priestess: I drink, yet it is not wine I drink but the blood of the Goddess, since from wine it has changed into her blood and spread itself through the growing vines and trees, fruit ripening under the moon. I drink and salute the moon, praying that the Goddess will guard the grape until the harvest is complete. May it be good!

Food Offerings and Libations

If the food has been made with intent and blessings, it becomes more than ordinary food, and thus makes a suitable offering to the Gods and spirits. When we bless the bread and wine, before we take any, we offer a portion to the Gods. Bread is thrown onto the fire so that its essence might be released to them with the words "The first is always for the Gods". A libation of wine is made in a similar manner. (A libation is a pouring of wine, milk or other drink onto the ground or before an image as an offering to the Gods.)

We always leave more food behind in the woods for the local spirits after the feast. In reality, of course, it is the animals and birds that eat it, but we consider that first the spirits consume its essence.

THE POWERS ARE THANKED

The beings who have attended are thanked for their help. They are offered a blessing before they depart.

THE CIRCLE IS DISMANTLED

When all is finished the circle is dissolved. Closing the rite properly is as important as opening it correctly. If you feel ill or unusually tired after a ritual, you have not done something right: either you have left open some of the gates that should be shut, like one of the quarters, or you have not earthed or directed the power that was raised accurately. If you don't close the power down, particularly if you are working in your own home, it will cause problems which may manifest in the form of odd noises, balls of light, smells and so on.

Take the knife and cut through the boundary of the circle near the east and say words to the effect of:

> *Mighty powers of the east, thank you for guarding our circle and for witnessing our rites. I bless you in the name of the Lord and the Lady* (or whatever deities you call upon).

Repeat in all the other directions. Cut through the centre and thank the powers of above and below. Put out the candles and dismantle the temple.

CLEARING AWAY

Everything used within a ritual should be considered a sacred object and treated with proper respect. Never throw any ritual equipment, including bread, candle stubs, wine or flowers, into the rubbish bin. If there is any wine or bread left over after your offerings and own use, pour the wine into the earth and leave the bread in the garden to be eaten by birds and wild creatures. Candles should be burned away. Always cleanse your ritual equipment immediately and put it away.

AFTERWARDS

The participants should be 'earthed' by eating and drinking. In addition to sharing the cakes and wine, it is the custom to share feasts at the festivals and other ritual occasions of the Pagan year. In the past, people were acutely aware of the passing of the seasons and what each had to offer in terms of food, herbs and animal behaviour. We live in a time when food is always available in the shops and we tend to forget the importance of the agricultural and pastoral year which was everything to our ancestors. The festivals of Paganism attempt to make us more aware of the natural cycles and our part in them. At our seasonal celebrations, and their accompanying feasts, we try to honour and reflect the connections of herbs and plants with the seasons.

When using ceremonial food, we must choose ingredients that are suitable for the time of year, that reflect its symbolism, that are appropriate to the time and place.[x] It is useful to find old traditional festival or seasonal recipes for this. We should take care that it is carefully prepared, with magical intent.

Rituals have meaning, and the resonances of those meanings may not become apparent until later. You may find that something fits into a pattern you have been perceiving, or supplies a piece of the Cosmic puzzle. Deeper and deeper meanings under what at first appeared simple and superficial will be revealed in the weeks following the ritual. Each participant may gain something different from the ritual, though at first glance their experiences may appear similar; we are given what we need at the time, according to our depth of understanding and progress.

Chapter 3
PUBLIC RITUALS

There are two types of group ritual: those of a coven/working magical group and public rituals where there may be beginners and people of different traditions.

Public rituals always fail to reach the levels of achievement of those of a working group or coven for obvious reasons. A close-knit working group has trained together, shares a tradition, uses common symbols, mythology and ritual formats and can balance the energy of each person within the ritual, melding into the group-mind. Each person is capable of contributing to the invocations, the raising of power and of recognising and working with spirit when it arrives; the group has forged its higher plane contacts and is capable of invoking them into the circle. With public rituals, little or none of this is true.

It isn't just a question of numbers. You can have a group of sixty people from the same tradition who know the symbolism and myths of the clan who, while they may not know each other well or work with each other more than a handful of times a year, can achieve a truly magical experience.

However, most public rituals have to cater for some individuals without even the most basic knowledge of a ritual format, myth or ritual behaviour, as well as a diverse collection of witches, Druids, Heathens and the undecided. Some people will join in enthusiastically, others will only stand and watch. How do you accommodate those who believe all gods are one god, those who believe in a god and goddess, those who literally believe in every god who has ever been named, those who believe in a variety of spirits and those who simply believe that the gods are fragmented portions of their own psyches? The danger here is that the ritual can become so diluted and generic in an attempt to encompass every possible stance and not offend anyone that it becomes anodyne and ineffectual. People who have only ever been to rituals of this kind may have no idea of what a ritual can be.

This does not mean that public rituals cannot be effective and powerful for those involved, but sadly, they rarely are.

SMALL PUBLIC RITUALS

Small public rituals are often held by Pagan moots and societies. By 'small' I mean under thirty or forty or so people. As with larger public rituals, they may involve people from different traditions, with different methods or practice, as well as solitaries who wish to take the opportunity to work with others. Group rituals are about people coming together by common consensus to celebrate, in spite of any differences of belief and approach. It requires participants to be willing to try new things and proceed according to the tenets of those hosting the event, mindful that not everything is going to be done exactly according to their own tradition. The vast majority of Pagans are willing to do this and it is a great tribute to their flexibility and open-mindedness that they can, and moreover, to the confidence of modern Paganism that it can encompass and welcome a wide variety of views. Yes, I know, there's always the chap in the corner moaning that they don't do it *this* way in *his* tradition so they're all wrong and therefore fluffy bunnies, but you can't please all of the people all of the time.

For this kind of group ritual, it is best if you can get most of the participants involved in planning it:

- Intent comes first, of course- what is the ritual for? A statement of intent is made at the beginning of the ritual so that everyone understands what they are there for. Writing this helps you crystallise what it is the ritual is all about.
- What does the group want to get out of the ritual?
- How will you make everyone feel involved?
- Do you have people with enough power and confidence to make the invocations? It is nice to give everyone the opportunity, but it is vital that the invocations are effective.
- How will you convey the theme of the ritual? You might use symbols and decorations that express the season; you might use poetry, songs, chants and stories, costumes and masks. Used well, such things can convey the meaning of the ritual on a deep level beyond the conscious mind. Decorating the ritual space and making masks, flower chaplets, corn dollies, decorated eggs and so on (depending on the season) can really help people tune into the ritual beforehand. The more preparation that people do, the better.
- Use music and circle dancing to raise the power. Ask everyone to bring drums, tambourines or something to make a noise with. Use a simple chant, not a long one that newcomers might not know.
- Try to avoid people making long invocations, charges etc read from pieces of paper, for reasons already explained in Chapter 2. It is much better that people say a few words from the heart. Consider using mime and ritual drama to convey the theme of the event.
- Try to include something that makes the ritual address each person's spiritual development. At Ostara, for example, you could hand out a seed to each person, explaining that it is the seed of their potential; it must be planted, watered and nurtured if it is to thrive.
- Try to give every person an opportunity to speak about what the festival means to them, and what they are seeking to gain from it – you might pass round a talking stick.

- A feast after the ritual is a good way to ground afterwards, to chat and celebrate. You can ask people to bring food to share, preferably seasonal food that they have made themselves. During the feast you can have poems, stories and songs on the theme of the ritual.

LARGE PUBLIC RITUALS

Rituals that work for a coven will not work for a larger group for obvious reasons. At one Pagan camp I went to, participants were instructed to spiral inwards and take a drink from the Cauldron of Ceridwen. This was a lovely idea, but three-hundred folk spiralling in (shuffling in) and trying to get to the cauldron took hours. People lost focus and started chatting. Some got fed up and wandered away. The next part of the ritual never happened at all and everything petered out without a proper closing.

Public rituals have to be carefully planned and orchestrated by a group of people willing to take responsibility for them. Waiting for it all to come together at the last minute never works. Throwing the ritual open for input while it is in progress is optimistic in the extreme. If you say "*Okay, we've created the ritual space, now it is up to you what you do,*" everyone will just stand around looking at each other getting more and more embarrassed. As with any other kind of ritual, you should be clear what the intent of the ritual is. This intent should be made clear to the participants and it is usual to have s statement of purpose at the beginning so that no one is in any doubt. Individuals can then focus on this object to the best of their abilities. If you aren't clear what you are asking for, how can the magic make it happen?

You might process to the ritual space, accompanied by music, drumming or chanting. This could involve travelling deosil around the circle once or three times before the procession stops.

If you can, try to have key people doing the invocations, people you know are capable of drawing Spirit into the circle rather than just someone who can say the words.

For a large public ritual, gestures have to be larger and more theatrical. Before you cry "*this is play-acting not ritual!*", let me remind you that originally, theatre was a way of honouring the Gods, and in traditional cultures, it still is. The word 'theatre' comes from the same root as 'theology', the Greek *theos*, meaning 'god'.[y] In Greece, theatre evolved from the ecstatic rites of the god Dionysus to become a public method of worship and reconnection to spirit which took place at the sacred centre of the community. There is no real distinction between ritual and ritual theatre, and one cannot be made by insisting that unless everyone present has a part, it is not ritual. This was never the way rituals were conducted in the ancient world or in traditional societies.

That said, every effort should be made to involve all the attendees, though you will get a variety of responses. On one occasion I witnessed, the priest calling the quarters announced that all the participants should join him and call the quarters in their own way. There were a few half-hearted mumblings in the east, silence in the south, and by the time we got to west the priest had given in and called the quarter in the usual manner, finishing with 'hail and welcome' and received a relieved response of 'hail and welcome' from the assembly. A more effective way of involving everyone in calling the quarters I saw was having everyone walk round to the quarters and bang drums in welcome after the invocations had been made. However, this won't work if you have more than about fifty people, or have a small space.

If the situation allows it (and it usually doesn't) you could try dividing the attendees into smaller groups to talk about, meditate on, and plan different parts of the ritual. You could even try to get them to work through a rite of purification before they come to the circle.

Theoretically, the power generated by three hundred people should be much greater than that generated by ten but it is usually not the case, simply because many participants have no clue how to do this, or even want to. You can try raising energy with drumming and chanting, but the chant will have to be very simple so that everyone can quickly catch on. If the space permits, you can incorporate movement and dance around the perimeter of the circle. Encouraging people to join hands to do this is good, and you might think about moving in spirals or a double circle. At the Wessex Gathering this year, to open the ritual, everyone walked around the circle, pausing in front of each other person to say "*One time, one place, one spirit*" and this meant we could all meet everyone else face to face, greet them, raise power and create community with the chant. Again, this would take too long with more than a hundred or so people.

If you are going to have bread and wine as part of the ritual, you have to make sure everyone gets some, and everything doesn't grind to a halt while you wait an hour or two for the chalice to get round five hundred people. We solve this at the Mercian Gathering by having four chalice bearers and four bread bearers who start off at the quarters who go round while the bard performs a song based on a charge or myth that fits in with the occasion.

Chapter 4
MAKING MAGIC

"If the essence and perfection of all good are comprehended in the gods, and the first and ancient power of them is with us priests (i.e. theurgists or magicians) and if by those who similarly adhere to more excellent natures and genuinely obtain a union with them, the beginning and end of all good is earnestly pursued; if this be the case, here the contemplation of truth, and the possession of intellectual science are to be found. And a knowledge of the Gods is accompanied with . . . the knowledge of ourselves."

Iamblichus, the Neoplatonist [z]

In Paganism ritual, worship and magic go hand in hand. Indeed, if we look at the history of most of the world's faiths, it is not possible to separate magic and religion.

INTENT AND REALITY

Magic is usually defined as the art and science of effecting changes in accordance to Will, to paraphrase Aleister Crowley; a means of influencing the world, the Cosmos and developing the Self using ritual, trance and symbolism. Crowley wrote:

"What is a Magical Operation? It may be defined as any event in nature which is brought to pass by Will. We must not exclude potato-growing or banking from our definition. Let us take a very simple example of a Magical Act: that of a man blowing his nose."[aa]

The important thing here is acting with intent, acting from true Will. Will is not the same thing as willpower; it is not the same thing as desire. Those things might be passing fancies generated by our subconscious fears and insecurities. The true Will is developed by knowing who and what you are and by understanding what the soul needs, not what the transient personality wants. A magical act must begin with clear intent, and that intent must come from true Will. Magical training begins and continues with understanding the difference between the transient personality and the soul, transcending what we have been shaped into by our negative life experiences, and reconnecting with the eternal soul.

As we grow up we are taught to limit our thoughts and ideas, our vision of what is possible. Yet it is only our thoughts which limit us; and we can control our thoughts. The brain processes 400 billion bits of information per second, but we are only aware of about 2000. The brain receives the rest of the information, but we don't integrate that knowledge; we are only aware of the tip of the iceberg when it comes to what the brain receives. Our eyes see far more than we process, but we only process and integrate the things we need, or which seem to be what we need or which fit in with what we expect to see. [ab]

When new things happen to us, they become part of our reality, part of our neural net. The brain firing thoughts is like a lightening cloud with electrical impulses moving through it. We can't see or measure a thought, but scientists can detect the storms raging in different parts of the brain. [ac]

We think that science has given us a view of the world that establishes a concrete reality, but much of science is theory designed to fit observed events, and these theories are continually revised. Newtonian physics gave us a mechanical view of the universe, solid objects reacting according to gravity and so on. Matter was thought of as static and predictable. We now know that the universe is not a concrete 'reality', and later theorists spoke in terms of energies. We don't know that black holes exist; they are a mathematical theory to explain certain observed phenomena. Sub atomic physics is nothing more than an idea that attempts to explain what is going on at a sub-atomic level.

Atoms (once thought to be the smallest unit of matter) are not solid. An atom is a particle of dense matter surrounded by a cloud of electrons. Matter takes up a tiny part of an atom, and the rest is a vacuum. (The universe, therefore, is not filled with solid objects- it is mostly empty, though the table in front of you seems to be solid, it is mostly empty space.) Moreover, the electrons pop in and out of existence, as does the nucleus itself. Where they go in between time is a big question, and some even speculate that they go into an alternative universe. Some have said that an atom is more like a thought than a solid speck of matter- it is made up of information. [ad]

A thousand years ago, you would have been laughed at for saying the earth was round, when everyone knew it was flat. Two hundred years ago you would have been hounded out of any scientific establishment for saying that time is flexible, but Einstein proved (by mathematical theory) that time is relative, and depends on the observer.

Quantum physics goes further, and according to its principles, it is possible not only to go forward in time, but also backwards. Laboratory experiments have proved that the same particle can be in two places at the same time simultaneously. According to quantum theory, reality only exists as potential until we observe it. We are used to thinking that things exist without our input, but they exist only as possible movements of consciousness. Things are not things, but tendencies. As we observe, we choose which possibility manifests. It has now been proved that the observer shapes the outcome of any experiment. In other words, reality in not concrete, but only one of many potentials. We create our own reality moment by moment.[ae]

In 1993 four hundred people went to Washington to meditate on reducing crime by 25%. Crime was reduced by 25%. Forty eight other studies and experiments in this area have shown the same results. We affect the reality we see. We are not victims of reality, but moment by moment create our own reality. We do this with our intent.

Water is the most receptive of all the elements. In Japan there was a polluted lake called Lake Biwa, covered with invading foul-smelling algae. On July 25th 1999 three hundred and fifty people gathered, led by Dr Shioya to pay and recite the Great Declaration: *"the infinite power of the universe takes shape and takes shape, the world became truly great and powerful"*. A month later most of the algae had gone. [af]

Also in Japan, Masaru Emoto has been conducting experiments with the effect of intent on water crystals. (These experiments have been duplicated and repeated thousands of times.) Beautiful frozen water crystals form after the words 'thank you' have been pasted on the jar of water, but the same water after the words 'you fool' have been pasted on the jar forms poor and distorted crystals. Intent has affected the structure of the water. If thoughts can do that to water, what can they do to us? 70% of our bodies is water. We can se already that this has implications for healing. Emoto theorises that water is sensitive to Hado, vibrational energy or universal energy that is elsewhere defined as Mana, Chi or Prana. 'Thank you' or 'you fool' carries its own vibrational energy, so that words and the intent behind them affect matter. [ag]

Holistic healers state that illness begins in the psyche, and that illness follows on from trauma, emotional upset, stress, rage and so on. When we project these emotions onto our body, illnesses follow. Trauma, stress and negative emotions trigger the disease process (anger causes arthritis and auto-immune diseases, conflict causes cancer and so on). In terms of quantum physics we are creating our own reality.

The body is not a solid object that carries you through life. It is a network of energy and information in dynamic exchange with the world around you. With every breath, every mouthful of food, every noise you hear and sight you see, your body changes. In the last few seconds, it has exchanged four hundred billion trillion atoms with your environment.[ah] The body only appears to be static because the changes taking place are too small to see. Every year 98% of the atoms have been exchanged. In three years every single atom is different. The body is an energy that exists in a constant state of transformation. At the deepest level of existence, we truly are one with the Cosmos.

So when we get a new liver every few months, why does a diseased liver renew itself with diseased cells? Because the body consciousness programmes it to. We expect it to happen, and so it does. It has been shown, over and over again, that people who expect to recover do so, and that people who have poor expectations deteriorate much faster and have a poorer prognosis. A sick person surrounded with stress, anger and negativity is having the sickness continually fed and exacerbated and will deteriorate fast. A sick person surrounded by calm, love and positivity can experience miracles.

We create our own realities by the stories we tell ourselves about what the outside world is. The brain uses the same neural net for experience and memory. It builds its concepts by memory and forges relationships between the different areas, so that love may be connected with pain, hurt with rage. We react to current situations as though they were the situations of the past, connection with those past emotions in a new situation. If you do this on a regular basis the nerve cells form a stronger connection between the two areas. Stop doing this and those connections weaken. We are our emotions. The mind creates the body - it starts in the cell which is given its signal by the brain. If it is bombarded over and over again by the same emotional chemicals, it looses sensitivity and the same amount of chemicals elicits a smaller response. If we are bombarding the cells with the same chemical or attitude day after day, when the cell is dividing the daughter cell will have more receptor sites for the chemical and less for vitamins, mineral and so on. This is how disease starts in the body.

People don't consciously affect themselves because they do not believe that they can. If you think you can achieve something you can. If you tell yourself you can't, you won't. We think we have no role in determining our own reality, that we are insignificant and the victim of circumstances when the reality is that we choose our experiences and determine our own reality. People can make different or better choices by intent. If you are bored or unhappy, you can, by intent, dispense with your addiction to this situation and make the decision to change your life. There are things that make you evolve, and things that don't, junctures in the path that allow for change or resigned acceptance. When we begin to make our own choices with intent, we accrue what is called Personal Power, i.e. magical power. According to the Egyptian Coffin Texts: "*The magician fills his belly with magic power; by its virtue he slakes his thirst.*" [ai]

The Magician's World View

We've already seen that for magic and ritual, we need to have a different view of the world and 'reality' than the one that is commonly accepted. For the Pagan, there is no real difference between matter and spirit, and there is no real separation between the individual and the Cosmos; gods, humans, and everything else are part of each other, indivisibly connected. For the Pagan, Divine Spirit is not separate from creation, but is manifest within it and within each of us; linked in a chain of cosmic union.

The philosopher and magician Francis Barrett said that "*Magic is a comprehensive knowledge of All Nature*" in other words, knowledge of how all things function. The magician's notion of the universe and its workings is not the same as that of the scientist or natural philosopher: the magician has a particular world-view in which knowledge is organised and interpreted in a certain way. He or she then follows natural laws in accordance with that knowledge.

To be capable of wielding occult power is a lifetime's work - it involves the striving for perfection on the part of the magician, what we in our tradition call the Grail Quest, but which others refer to as Great Work or Soul Quest. The Renaissance magician Cornelius Agrippa once posed the question as to how it was possible for a man to wield magical powers, and then answered himself:

> *"No one has such powers but he who has cohabited with the elements, vanquished nature, mounted higher than the heavens, elevating himself above the angels to the archetype itself, with whom he then becomes co-operator and can do all things".*[aj]

The ultimate aim of any serious magician is not the childish creation of effects, but the realization of his or her full mental powers, the freeing of the spirit from the chains of ego and the material realm so that it might pass freely through the universal doors and know what is unknowable in the normal course of life. This expansion of knowledge, of consciousness, this striving to achieve perfect balance – nothing less than the fundamental transformation of the Self - is the ultimate aim of magic and ritual. A person who has fully experienced the unity of him or herself with the Cosmos is said to have completed the Great Work or to have achieved the Holy Grail:

> *"In each sentient being there awakens a heart which is the heir of the divine heart. It holds the divine power, and answers for the righteousness of the magician as he faces his judges…It is for the magician to develop his intuitive faculties which allow him to discover the mysterious casket of knowledge…His heart will tell him how to open it, so that he may find the essence of magic…the purpose of magic is to make a heart of heavenly origin beat within him, to awaken his perception of the invisible."* [ak]

The main purpose of Pagan magic is linking to the Gods, developing the magician and bringing the power and will of the Gods onto the physical plane, heightening awareness, increasing knowledge. Thus magic has been the way of spiritual growth in the mystery schools. Using magic and ritual, we can connect with the powers of the Cosmos, with spirits of all levels, and through direct experience, we understand the workings of the universe.

Many Pagans think of magic as the thread that links the Cosmos. Christian Jacq, in his study of Egyptian magic, said that:

> "*…magic can perhaps be defined as the essential energy that flows through both the divine and human spheres.*" [al]

To practice magic, we must identify this linking thread. Magic has always been seen as a creative force. In many mythologies, it is said to have been in existence before creation, and creation is a manifestation of magic.

The fundamental building blocks of the universe are not atoms. Matter and energy are interchangeable. Matter is slowed down, crystallised energy. The physical body is energy. The universe is a web of energy patterns, constantly moving and constantly changing. Nothing can be truly described as being separate from anything else. The Cosmos is holistic.

Occultists and healers maintain that an aura surrounds the entire human body and that a web of energy permeates the Cosmos. The concept a Cosmic Energy Field is at least 5,000 years old and is extant in a hundred or more cultures including Buddhist, Hindu, Rosicrucian and Native American teachings. The Chinese speak of an energy called Chi, which infuses all matter while the Indians speak of Prana, the life-breath which energises all living things.

Throughout the ages, scientists have investigated this universal energy. The alchemist Paracelsus called it Illiaster and said it was composed of both vital energy and vital matter. In the 19th century Count von Reichenbach called the energy 'odic force' and experimented with it for over thirty years. He determined that unlike electromagnetism, with the odic force like attracts like (an important principle independently expounded by magicians and healers). In the 20th century a psychiatrist called Wilhelm Reich called this energy 'orgone' and according to his observations any disturbance to the flow of orgone in the human body led to physiological or mental illness.

The Cosmic Energy field permeates everything, flowing continually from one thing to another. When something vibrates at a certain frequency, any object near it will begin to vibrate with the same frequency, a principle used both in healing and in magic.

THE LAWS OF MAGIC

At its core, there is a consistency in magical practice and thought all over the world, from the ancient cultures of Egypt and Babylon, and the shamans of Siberia and South America, to the mediaeval cabalist or modern witch. The laws of magic have been observed and codified by adepts over thousands of years.

Law 1: As Above So Below

This fundamental law of magic was inscribed on the Emerald Tablet of Hermes Trismegistus, one of the legendary magicians of the ancient world. It is said to have been discovered by Alexander the Great in the magician's tomb, and was inscribed in Phoenician script *"that which is above is like that which is below, and that which is below is like that which is above, to achieve the wonder of the one thing"*. The 'one thing' is the totality of which we have already spoken: the Unity, the Cosmos of which the physical universe is but a manifestation. All aspects of the Cosmos are reflections of 'one thing' which underlies and connects them. [am] What the tablet tells us is that what happens in the greater Cosmos is reflected here in the physical realm; events on Earth run parallel to events in the greater Cosmos because both are part of the One. This is the basis of such arts as astrology and divination, where the warp and weft of the greater pattern are discerned within specific threads such as the movement of the planets, the flight of a raven, or the fall of a tarot card.

It follows that what affects a small part of the Cosmos eventually affects the whole in some way. By manipulating events below in specific and powerful ways known to those who have studied them, the greater pattern will be affected - and this is the basis of magic.

The principle of above and below is sometimes referred to as the macrocosm and the microcosm. Macrocosm is from the Greek and means 'great arrangement' while microcosm means 'little world' or 'small arrangement'. The macrocosm refers to the Cosmos, which means not only the physical universe, but the totality of the One. Strictly speaking, the microcosm refers to the individual human, said to be a reflection of the principles of the macrocosm, a miniature cosmos. [1] By the same token, the macrocosm is viewed as a human organism on massive scale, and everything that humans experience is thought to be mirrored with greater magnitude in the universe.

Law 2: Like Attracts Like

According to the principles of magic, like is attracted to like; this is an extension of the principle as above so below. As Plotinus the Neo-Pythagorean explained: "*And how are magical operations (goêteias) carried out? By Sympathy, and thanks to the fact that there is a natural Harmony between things that are alike and a natural Opposition between things that are unlike*".

In a magic spell, or in a ritual, we will use something that is like a thing (an object, symbol, or action) to attract or influence that thing. For example, to attract rain, a tribal medicine man may pour water from a gourd, or by damaging a wax poppet in the likeness of a man, a sorcerer may seek to harm his enemy. In all cases, there must be a link established between the substitute and the target to make sure that the magic flies true. In the latter example, this may be done by naming the poppet for the victim (a person's name is part of their essence), or by incorporating his nails or hair into it so that what happens to part of the man will affect the whole of the man – working on the principle of microcosm and the macrocosm.

1 Who at death is reunited with the macrocosm.

On a basic level of operation, this is sometimes called sympathetic magic. A shaman may take a shell or bead that resembles the human eye and make it into an amulet to protect the bearer from the evil eye. A sufferer with an affected arm might leave a small model of an arm at the temple of a healing deity; a lame man might leave a bronze foot and so on. In Crete I saw many such historical offerings on display at the museum in Heraklion, but what I did not expect to see were identical tokens nearby in a modern day church on the island of Spinalonga, an old leper colony, left to implore the local saint for aid. Even today, in parts of Britain and Ireland, pieces of cloth are left at holy healing wells, tied to 'cloutie trees' so that when the cloth decays, the disease will disappear with it. (Those despoilers of the environment who tie bits of indestructible plastic to the trees are in for a disappointment.)

The use of analogy and representation brings us on to symbolism. A symbol is something that represents something else by being connected with it, an extension of the like to like principle: a statue or a glyph may be the symbol of a god, bread may symbolise food and nourishment, the rune beorc symbolises springtime, growth and feminine power. The colour green is associated with vegetation and growth, so a ritual for growth and expansion may make use of the colour green. Red is the colour of blood, and blood is necessary for life, so a spell for strength might make use of the colour red.

A symbol or image can convey ideas much more profoundly than any number of words and explanations; it appeals to the psyche on all levels. The subconscious mind communicates in the form of symbols and is the messenger between the physical and the spiritual realms. The psychologist Carl Jung said that

> "*The unconscious knows more than the conscious does; but it is a knowledge of a special sort, knowledge in eternity, usually without reference to the here and now, not couched in the language of intellect.*" [an]

Symbolism is the universal magical language. However, a symbol, as used in magic, is much more than a reference to a thing. When properly employed, it taps into the nature and essence of the thing itself: the form becomes the channel for its energy. The symbol takes on a level of actuality and participates in the magical reality. When we, with knowledge and intent, use a cauldron to represent the Cauldron of Ceridwen, it becomes her cauldron. The magical tools are focussing points which enable the ritualist to link with the spiritual force behind the symbol, which can stand for a complex and extended set of ideas: the cup stands for love, nurture, the emotions, the Grail and so on.

Symbols are keys that open the conscious mind to a collection of related ideas. Thus a ceremonial magician would associate the colour red with the Mars (the planet of strength and direct action) and a Mars ritual to invoke these energies might employ red candles and red robes. In my own tradition, red is the colour of energy, fire, the south and noonday, and for this reason we place a red candle in the south of the magic circle, so that every time we see it, we are reminded of these things.

Related correspondences or harmonics are used to reinforce the idea and add another layer of symbolism. Fire and the south are associated with the magical tool the wand and with the development of the Will. A simple red candle, placed in the south of the circle can bring all these resonances to mind. Elements, directions, festivals, gods and goddesses and states of mind have their own perfumes associated with them; every plant has a body of lore associated with it, and various uses in healing and in magic, affecting their blending and usage.

Using the harmonics of symbolism can become very complicated, and is best taken a step at a time. Become completely conversant with one set of symbols before adding the next layer and its concomitant associations. When you work with these ideas frequently further harmonics become apparent. We call these harmonics 'correspondences' and use them to set up the magical frequency we require for our intended purpose.

The vibration or wavelength of colours, images, smells and so on all reflect each other to create a harmonious whole. They should be consistent, whether simple or complex, each re-informing the intent. This helps to evoke and direct the right emotional response and level of consciousness in all the participants. There should be no jarring note that will detract from the overall goal or throw it off course.

It will have occurred to you that there are many possible interpretations of a single symbol. For the Hindu, a swastika is a symbol of good luck and the movement of the sun. For most people in the western world, on the other hand, it is associated with fascism and great evil. Any religious or magical system uses a codified system of symbols based on their own mythology and associations which all of their members learn and follow, but which outsiders do not (this in itself helps to bind a group or tradition). This does not mean that there is only one correct way of interpreting a symbol; it only means that any one group must use the same set. Introducing inconsistent elements or contradictory meanings into a symbolic system undermines the whole system. Using those symbols then weakens the power and cohesive nature of the tradition, blurs and obstructs its channels of Cosmic communication, and will eventually destroy it. Only the ignorant ever mix traditions, symbolic systems and pantheons, thus creating ritual chaos. Stick to symbols, traditions and pantheons you identify with.

Law 3: The Law of Balance and the Doctrine of Opposites

Like the modern Pagan, the ancient Greeks recognised polarities in nature: day and night, summer and winter, life and death and so on, a pendulum swinging back and forth. They believed, as we do, that those opposites are held in a kind of dynamic equilibrium, or eternal balance, by the Cosmic whole. This is characterised by the concept the Greeks called 'Justice', which is portrayed in the tarot card of that name. The ancient Egyptians called it *maat*, and it was embodied in the goddess Maat, the personification of truth, justice, divine order, cosmic harmony and balance, whose attributes include the scales, still a symbol of balance and justice today. It was the pharaoh's duty to maintain the rule of Maat, and Egyptian social organisation was meant to be a reflection of the divine and natural order. If the pattern should be transgressed against, then chaos and its consequences would follow. Maat's law governed all the worlds and even the gods had to obey her rule.

The path to the One lies in the reconciliation of opposites and their synthesis transcends them; the God and Goddess are reconciled in the whole. Some magicians purposely set out to experience the extremes of joy and sorrow, lust and chastity etc. in order to be able to know them and bring them into balance. Whether of not this is necessary, the initiate must try to bring about some measure of equilibrium of the opposing forces in his or her own nature: between intellect and emotion, the physical and the spiritual, the male and female sides of the personality and so on. One aspect should not be rejected in favour of the other. When balance and harmony are lost, then depression, negativity, conflict and illness result.

Pagans always strive to maintain the natural balance of the Cosmos itself, and this is sometimes achieved by using magic. The village wise woman was the first person a man or woman in trouble would turn to as the witch would understand what had happened to disturb the natural order of things, and see what had to be done to put it right. Witches were the healers, but not just of human bodies, but of the whole Cosmic harmony. This maintenance of balance applies to the giving and receiving of magical energies. The old Pagans knew that in order to receive, one must first give. When people wanted good crops, they made offerings to the gods of what they had – bread, wine and incense, for example. This is forgotten today when people demand without giving in return, even from the Gods.

Chapter 5
THE ELEMENTS

In modern Pagan magic we work with the four elements of earth, air, fire and water. These are not elements as defined by the periodic table, but four principles of energy. They come not from Semitic monotheistic magick, as many assume, but from ancient Pagan philosophy.

The early Greeks debated the composition of the world. Thales, looking around and seeing the plentiful nature of water, considered that it was the basic element of creation. In contrast, Heraclitus concluded it was fire and Anaxagoras thought it must be air. The four elements as the basic building blocks of creation were first defined by Empedocles, a fifth century BCE philosopher from Sicily who was an initiate of several mystery traditions. His *Tetrasomia* or 'Doctrine of the Four Elements' influenced Western philosophy and magic in the succeeding millennia. He didn't actually call these four principles 'elements' (*stoikheia*), but 'roots' (*rhizai*), since he was a magical herbalist. [ao] For him, the elements were not just physical forms but manifested spiritual essences or even god energies; they were the fourfold roots of everything which had existed in fixed quantities since the beginning of the universe, not as isolated things, but part of the whole.

EARTH

Earth is the densest of all the elements, solid like the bones that structure our bodies; indeed, rocks, stones and crystals are often seen by Pagans as the bones of Mother Earth. Earth is generally fixed, unlike the other elements which are mobile. From the stuff of the earth grows all living things and its immense nurturing power can sustain the greatest oak tree and the tiniest flower. [ap] It is associated with the material and the practical, the physical world and crystallized energy. What we do to the earth, we do to ourselves, since we are connected with it. We are rooted in the physical realm; it links us to who we are, to the past, to our ancestors, to our land.

Empedocles associated Earth with Hera *pheresbios* or 'life-bringing,' a traditional epithet of earth goddesses.[aq] She was the patroness of faithful marriage and stable social order, the fertility of women and nature. She was married to Zeus the sky god as Lord (*Hêrôs*) and Lady (*Hêra*). The pairing of earth and sky is a common one in mythology, the Hindu earth and mother goddess Prithvi Mata ('Mother Earth') compliments Dyaus Pita ("Father Sky") for example, and it is the mating of earth and sky that brings life.

The powers of earth are concerned with what is manifest, the material, the fixed, the solid, the practical, with what is rooted. Earth elemental magic might be concerned with manifestation, business, health, practicality, wealth, stability, grounding and centring, agriculture.

People who have a lot of earth in their psychological make-up are practical, stable, hard-working, dextrous and reliable, determined, patient, logical and ambitious. However, too much earth can manifest as laziness, bigotry, gluttony, pedantry, snobbery, clumsiness, stubbornness and inflexibility.

EARTH CORRESPONDENCES:

Key Words: darkness, returning, coldness, winter, rest and peace, foundation, permanence, structure, crystallisation, silence

Qualities: Physical, practical, stable, solid, grounded, responsible, objective, rooted, materialised.

Negative Qualities: Inflexible, rigid

Elementals: Gnomes

Cardinal Point: North

Festival: Yule

Time: Midnight

Colour: Green

Tool: Pentacle

Symbols: Crystals, fur, coins, stone, bone, mirror, shield, tree

Sense: Touch

Signs: Taurus, Virgo, Capricorn

Planets: Venus, Saturn, Earth

Tattwas: Prithivi

Alchemical Symbol: A downward pointing triangle bisected by a horizontal line

Tarot: The suit of pentacles

Gems: Green moss agate, emerald, green jasper, jet, malachite, olivine, peridot, green tourmaline, turquoise.

Metal: Lead, iron

Animals: Burrowing animals, stag, boar, bull, sow, bear and snake, mole, fox, rabbit, goat, hibernating creatures, dragons, mythic animals

Musical Instrument: Drums

Musical note: F

Vowel Sound: A

Herbs: Patchouli, vervain, honeysuckle, mugwort, fern, vertivert, primrose, horehound

Magical Influences: manifestation, practicality, health, wealth, crystals, image magic

AIR

The connections between air and spirit are many. 'Spirit' is derived from the Latin *spiro*, meaning 'I breathe'. 'Wind,' 'breath' and 'spirit' were believed by many peoples to be identical. In Egyptian mythology, the god Khnûmû or Kneph was a wind god, his name meaning 'wind/breath/spirit' or 'the air of life'. In Memphis, the chief god was Her-shef and the north wind, which issued from his nostrils, gave life to every living being. In several creation myths, it is the movement of air/ spirit across the grosser elements of earth and water that engender creation. In Greek myth, when humans were created from mud (water and earth) they were animated by Prometheus' gift of fire, but not completed until Athene breathed spirit into them.

There was a common idea that it is the air that separates the earth from the sky. In Egyptian myth, the air god Shu separated Nut the sky goddess from Geb the earth god. Air is what separates individual things, but it unites them through breath. The air you breathe is the air I breathe, and through it we are joined. The Pythagoreans thought that the Cosmos itself breathed, and this breathing created time and number, limiting the unlimited. The breathing of the Cosmos unites our individual breaths and binds our individual spirits into one.

Breath is a divine gift, returned to the giver at death. The secret of breath is part of the magic of air. We take air into us which contains vital energy that some call prana (which means both 'breath' and 'spirit') and others chi/qi among other names. When we breathe in deeply we inhale this life force and rhythmic breathing exercises helps to attune you to the powers of air.

Inhaled air is the sustaining breath of life, while exhaled air carries the words, poetry, and song that communicate human ideas and knowledge. In many myths creation is brought to life when a god breathes into it. It was often thought that spirit could be blown into or out of people and shamans employ a technique of blowing demons out of people.

The powers of air are concerned with the intellect, the powers of the mind, knowledge (as opposed to wisdom), logic, inspiration, information, teaching, memory, thought and communication. Like the other elements, the powers of air can be constructive or destructive. The gentle breeze cools and brings the life giving rain, but it can become the destructive hurricane. It is for this reason that the magical symbol of air is a two-edged sword.

People who have air dominant in their psychological make-up are flexible, versatile, dextrous, tasteful, idealistic, original, individual and tolerant. However, they can also be distant, self opinionated, easily bored, impatient, self-deceiving, superficial, indecisive, quarrelsome, manipulative, thoughtless, cruel, fickle, inconsistent, unreliable and two-faced.

AIR CORRESPONDENCES

Key Words: movement, inception, inspiration, planning, communication, knowledge.
Qualities: Intellect, mind, knowledge, reasoning, communication, inception, beginning, birth, first breath, vocalisation, emergence, planning, understanding.
Negative Qualities: fickleness
Elementals: Sylphs
Cardinal Point: East
Festival: Ostara
Time: Sunrise
Colour: Yellow
Tool: Athame
Symbols: Eggs, feathers, sword
Sense: Hearing
Signs: Aquarius, Libra, and Gemini
Planets: Mercury, Neptune
Tattwas: Waju
Alchemical Symbol: upward pointed triangle bisected by an horizontal line
Tarot: Suit of Swords
Gems: topaz, aventurine, mica, fluorite, citrine
Metal: tin
Animals: Butterflies, eagle, hawk and birds
Musical Instrument: Wind instruments
Musical note: E
Vowel Sound: E
Herbs: lavender, lemongrass, verbena, marjoram, mint, acacia, almond, benzoin, gum mastic
Magical Influences: the non-tangible affecting the tangible, psychism, mental ability, protection prophecy, visualization

FIRE

Fire is the most mysterious of all the elements. It seems almost supernatural in comparison to earth, air or water, which are states of matter while fire is energy. Fire is concerned with creativity, life energy and zeal. Fire generates illumination within, the light of the spirit. Fire gives us vitality, igniting action, animation and movement. It sparks courage and acts of bravery. It heats passion and enthusiasm. Fire is the power of inner sight and creative vision, directing it and controlling it to make it manifest in the world, the power of Will; according to Empedocles fire is the agent of action.

It is the glow of the candle flame, the warmth of the hearth, the burning heat of the desert, the incandescence of the sun. However, fire consumes. Fire is wild and untameable, dangerous; it can burn those around it.

Fire is an agent of transformation- the food in the cauldron is changed as it cooks, raw ores and metals are altered into useful objects on the blacksmith's forge, it is the alchemist's element of change, and it converts the materials it consumes into ashes. Cattle were driven over the ashes of the Beltane and Samhain fires to purify them, and flaming torches were carried around the crops at Midsummer to protect them.

Fire symbolises the life force. It was associated with the fertility of the land, and the ashes of the sacred fires were scattered on the land, to transfer the vigour of the fire spirits into the earth. It was also connected with the fertility of humans. Young men would leap through the festival fires to increase their virility, and young women jumped to become fertile. Fire magic is concerned with action and will. Fire corresponds to energy, power, passion, vitality.

People with a preponderance of fire in their make-up are energetic, vital, passionate, creative, intuitive, generous, courageous, driven, friendly, enterprising, philanthropic, warm, cheerful and honourable. However, they can also be ostentatious, arrogant, excessive, dominating, vain, promiscuous, aggressive, tactless and opinionated.

The spirit of the hearth fire is often thought of as a goddess. In Greek myth she was Hestia. Her name, according to Plato, means 'the essence of things'; a formless essence symbolised by the flame, which flows through everything that has life. She presided over all hearth and altar fires, and she was worshipped every day with prayers offered to her before and after meals. Her hearth was in the care of the woman of the home and before each meal something was thrown on the fire as an offering.

In Celtic lore, the goddess of the hearth is Brighid. She was invited into the home by the woman of the house, in the form of a doll or corn dolly dressed in maiden white. Oracles were taken from the ashes of the hearth fire, which people examined for a sign that Brighid had visited, i.e. a mark that looked like a swan's footprint; if found, it was a lucky omen (the swan was an ancient attribute of the goddess Brighid). Many Irish homes still have a Brighid's cross hung up. This four equal-armed cross was originally a solar symbol.

There is a connection between trades that use fire and magic. The magical reputation of the smith persisted in Europe into the nineteenth century and is still extant in India and Africa. In Britain, it was believed that smiths were blood charmers (healers) and could foretell the future. Even the water the smith used to cool metal had magical properties and was much sought after for healing purposes. A smithy-forged nail, hammered into a tree, was thought to transfer the illness to the tree. Smiths also possessed the secret of the Horseman's Word which, when whispered into the ear of the wildest horse, would calm it. People swore oaths by the smith's anvil and in some places he had the authority to marry couples, as at the famous Gretna Green in Scotland. In fairy stories smiths often protect people and animals against malignant fairies, evil spirits, witchcraft, and the evil eye.

The Greeks thought we each contained a part of the celestial fire. Prometheus created humans by mixing earth and water to create the body, Athena spirit into it, but Prometheus added fire, the higher soul.

The fire in the heavens, the sun, also had a counterpart in the underworld – the volcanic fires beneath the earth, the realm of the sun as it enters underworld on the same path taken by the dead, shining on the dark realm as it passes through. It is known as the Dark Sun, the Black Sun, the Invisible Sun, the Subterranean Sun and the Volcanic Sun.

FIRE CORRESPONDENCES

Key Words: energy, directing, illuminating, transforming, illumination
Qualities: Will, Energy, force, life, passionate, warmth, activity, expansion, courage, motion, blood, vitality, tenacity, strong, directing
Negative Qualities: destructive, devouring, aggressive
Elemental: Salamanders
Cardinal Point: South
Festival: Midsummer
Time: Noon
Colour: Red
Tool: Wand
Symbols: candles, torches
Sense: Smell
Signs: Leo, Aries, Sagittarius
Planets: Mars, Sun, Pluto
Tattwas: Tejas
Alchemical Symbol: upward pointing triangle
Tarot: The Suit of Wands
Metals: brass, gold
Gems: red agate, amber, bloodstone, carnelian, citrine, quartz, diamond, garnet, red jasper, lava, ruby, sard, sardonyx, sunstone, topaz, red tourmaline
Animals: Salamanders, lions, lizards
Musical Instrument: Voice
Musical note: D
Vowel Sound: I

Herbs: Allspice, frankincense, ginger, juniper, marigold, orange, rosemary, dragon's blood, clove, bay, ash
Magical Influences: active energy, illumination, wisdom, willpower, passion, healing,

WATER

Water has often been considered to be a living thing, or certainly to have the power of sustaining, bestowing and even restoring life- as well as being capable of taking it. Every ancient society honoured springs, wells, and water sources as sacred. The Celts and others sacrificed treasure to lake and river spirits. Rivers were worshipped by the Druids and were believed to each have their resident water spirits that required sacrifices to be made to them. The River Tweed is said to demand a yearly sacrifice, but the Till is more voracious, demanding two.

Just as water takes the form of whatever it is poured into, water gods and spirits have the power to alter their shape. A 'prototype' of water spirits is the Greek sea god Proteus, known as The Old Man of the Sea, who is the most masterful shapeshifter of all. He is able to assume any shape he desires. Most water spirits are said to be shapeshifters, perhaps because of the fluid and changeable nature of water itself, which is only given shape by the vessel that holds it.

Water is liquid, like the blood that flows through our veins. Water can manifest in a drop of dew, a gentle rain to the raging flood or the crash of the ocean wave. A trickle of water will eventually wear away a mountain. All life started in the rich biological soup of the oceans, just as the uterine waters of your mother's womb protected you. It is associated with emotions and feelings, the subconscious mind. Water can be the safety of the uterine waters of the womb, the cleansing stream, the deep pool of the subconscious mind, the nourishing river, the brew of initiation, the movement of the tides and the power of the sea to give bounty or destroy with its tempest.

Water is a universal symbol of cleansing and regeneration. Some bodies of water have healing powers, like the Chalice Well in Glastonbury. Water heals; especially water that flows east to west is empowered by the rising sun at the vernal equinox, May Day and Midsummer. Any stream that runs north to south has magical properties as does the place where two streams meet; these were often the places for magic and Otherworld contact. Pools and lakes are magical entrances to the Otherworld. Where three streams meet was always considered to be a especially potent place for magic where people gathered to drink the water as it had magical properties.

Water is ruled by the moon which pulls the ebb and flow of the tides, and many water spirits are said to appear by moonlight. Under the full moon is the best time to contact them. Our bodies too respond to the moon's tides, as they are mainly water. We are influenced by the moon tides almost as much as water elementals, though more subtly. Water relates to the ebb and flow of events, the natural tides of life.

People with a lot of water in the psychological make-up can be idealistic, romantic, psychic, artistic, poetic, nurturing and imaginative. However, they can also be self-involved, selfish, vapid, avaricious, ruthless, indecisive, manipulative, weak, over emotional and impractical.

WATER CORRESPONDENCES

Key Words: culmination, harvest, flowing, nourishing, love, intuition, .emotions, feelings, intuition, compassion, empathy, sympathy, devotion, quest, aspiration, harmony, beauty, serenity, fluidity, joy.

Qualities: Emotions, receptive, instinctive, compassionate, unconscious, psychic, mystic, flowing,

Negative Qualities:: Over emotional, disintegrating, dissolving, secretive, ungrounded, forgetful, clouded

Elemental: Undines

Direction: West

Colour: blue

Tool: cup

Symbols: cup, cauldron, pool, mirror, seashells

Sense: Taste

Signs: Cancer, Scorpio, Pisces

Planets: Moon, Venus, Neptune

Tattwas: Apas

Alchemical Symbol: downward pointing triangle

Stones: Pearl, Aquamarine, Moonstone,

Metal: Quicksilver, silver

Animal: Fish, dolphins, whales, all aquatic creatures

Musical instrument: String instruments

Musical note: g

Vowel Sound: O

Herbs: Aloe, apple, lemon balm, belladonna, birch, poplar, poppy, blackberry, burdock, camphor, chamomile, elder, ragwort, rose, coltsfoot, comfrey, daisy, daffodil, datura, sandalwood, yarrow, elm, eucalyptus, foxglove, hemlock, hemp, hibiscus, jasmine, yew, spearmint, thyme, kava-kava, ladies slipper, lemon, myrrh, morning glory, passion flower

QUALITIES AND HUMOURS

Aristotle (384-322 BCE) developed a different explanation for the elements based on pairs of qualities - warm, cold, dry and moist, represented by the Elemental Square which depicts the four elements and the powers between them, since the elements are mixtures of two powers. Earth is dry and cool, water is cool and moist, air is moist and warm and fire is warm and dry, though in each element, one power is dominant; earth is predominantly dry, water predominantly cool, air predominantly moist, and fire predominantly warm. [ar]

Like the elements, the powers manifest in many ways. According to the Pythagoreans, there is a natural progression they called the Organic Cycle: *"The first phase of growth is Moist: spring rains, pliant green shoots, rapid growth. The second phase is Warm: summer sun, flourishing individuality, mature vigour. The third is Dry: autumn leaves, inflexible stems, stiffening joints. The fourth is Cool: winter chills, loss of identity, death."* [as]

The notion that health depended on the balance of the four elements arose shortly after Empedocles introduced his theory. The theory of the four humours within the body had developed by the time of Hippocrates (c.460-c.377 BC) and it was thought that health depended on a balance of them: fire corresponded to blood and sanguinity; air to yellow bile and choler; water to phlegm and phlegmatic and earth to black bile and melancholy.

ELEMENTALS

The Neoplatonists, in the third century CE, spoke of spirits associated with each of the elements, and divided them into four classes, each associated with one of the elements. However, it was the sixteenth century alchemist, doctor and philosopher Paracelsus who gave these elementals their familiar names.[at] He called the spirits of the earth Gnomes, the spirits of the air Sylphs, spirits of fire Salamanders and water spirits Undines.

According to Paracelsus, while Sylphs and Undines are kindly disposed towards humans, Salamanders cannot be approached or approach humans, and Gnomes are usually malevolent. However, Gnomes can be persuaded to become servants to a magician and "*if you do your duty to him, he will do his duty to you.*" He went on to say that elementals hate dogmatists, sceptics, drunkards, gluttons, and the quarrelsome, while they love natural, child-like, innocent, and sincere people. "*...to him who binds or pledges himself to them they give knowledge and riches enough. They know our minds and thoughts also, so that they may be easily influenced to come to us.*"

Paracelsus declared that while man is made of three substances - the spiritual, the astral and terrestrial - elementals live exclusively in only one of the elements. They occupy a position between men and pure spirits, though they have blood and bones, they eat and sleep and mate and produce offspring. They live in dwellings that are made of special materials *"as different from the substances we know as the web of a spider is different from our linen".* The powers and influences of each the four elements are embodied in its elementals. Elementals are specialized spirits concerned with their own spheres of influence, and have no great interest in human affairs.

Pagans work with elementals, inviting them into the circle or ritual space. One of the basic principles that any witch or shaman learns is that almost everything in the Cosmos is made up of some combination of the four elements. If you can know the four elements directly, then you can understand anything in the Cosmos.

Working with elementals is fraught with danger, and they must be treated with the utmost respect. Any requests for their help must be carefully phrased, since they tend to take things literally, and properly directed to the correct type of elemental. Earth elementals are concerned with the physical world, with growth, formation, strength and health. Earth elemental magic might include working with plants, crystals, gardens, and the wildwood. Air elementals are concerned with movement, communication, the psychic senses, inspiration, and the powers of the intellect. Fire elementals are concerned with passion, transformation, purification, and energy. Water elementals are concerned with the ebb and flow, with tranquillity, purification, cleansing, scrying, and the emotions. The most usual representation for the elemental in ritual is a stone for the earth elemental, a feather or incense for the air elemental, a candle for the fire elemental, and a cauldron of water for the water elemental.

THE FIFTH ELEMENT

Plato developed the concept of an incorruptible fifth element called *aithêr* or *aether*, referring to the eternal heavens. The Pythagoreans used the initial letters of these five elements to name the outer angles of their symbol, the pentagram.

We can find widespread evidence of this five element system around the world, though whether it spread from Greece or developed independently in some places is impossible to prove.

In ancient India, for example, there was fire (*agni*), water (*ap*) and earth (*prithivi*). Fire was seen as emanating from air (*vâyu*), which emanates from aether (*âkâsha*). The classical elements in Hinduism are *Bhoomi* (Earth), *Jala* (Water), *Agni* (Fire), *Vayu* (Air) and *Akasa* (Space).[au]

The Chinese also had a five element system which is thought to predate Buddhism and was first expounded by Tsou Yen (350 - 270 BCE). They are wood, fire, earth, metal, and water. In traditional Chinese philosophy, the five elements are translated as five phases, five movements or five steps, by which all natural phenomena can be explained. Wood burns and gives rise to fire, which produces ash (earth), which contains metal. Metal attracts dew (water) which nourishes wood and so on. Alternatively, wood, in the form of a plough, overcomes earth, which constrains water, which quenches fire. Fire liquefies metal and metal cuts wood. The five primary colours are also associated with the five elements, the five compass directions (north, south, east, west and centre), the seasons, five compound colours, and a host of others attributes.

Buddhist temples are designed to symbolise the five elements: fire, air, earth, water and wisdom, symbolised by the pinnacle at the top. The fifth element is sometimes given as void or space since the Sanskrit word *akasa*, used for aether, can also mean 'sky' or 'clear space.'

Pagans think of the fifth element as being spirit or quintessence.

Chapter 6
MAGICAL TOOLS

When you create a magical tool, it is the material manifestation of an act of magic. Each tool should be made with intent, in the correct manner, and infused with magical power so that you experience its properties, and make it part of you. If you cannot forge your own sword it must be won, the wand must be cut and made by the user, and the pentacle should be inscribed by the user. In the Craft, the cup is given as a gift at the first degree initiation. Together they represent the four elemental powers.

In different traditions, which tool represents each element varies. We use the cup for west and water, the pentacle for north and earth, the knife for east and air, and the wand for south and fire. Others may use a different system in which the knife is south and fire, and the wand is east and air, for example. There is no right or wrong way, just use a system you understand and which is consistent.

THE CUP

The symbolism of the cup is many layered. On one level the cup is a similar tool to the cauldron, representing the nurturing and loving womb of the Goddess; it contains, holds and protects and the sharing of the cup during a ritual exemplifies this. When we drink we make a direct connection with Mother Nature, harking back to our very first sustenance, mother's milk. Both the milk and the cup are also mythically connected to the goddess of the moon, which is seen as a vessel filled with physical and emotional food for the world: one which empties and is replenished every month, ever nurturing. Both the cauldron and the cup possess this power of replenishment and regeneration.

The liquid that fills the ritual cup is wine, brewed from the life energy of a plant, matured under the moon which measures the time of its fermentation. It is a drink which gives inspiration, vitality and which changes the consciousness. The cup demonstrates the need to satisfy the thirst for both the liquid nourishment of the earth and the desire for spiritual knowledge. Those who have never felt thirst can never know the joy of its quenching.

The cup corresponds to the element of water and the season of autumn. In Celtic myth it was brought from the mystical city of Murias. Its station on the wheel is Herfest, the autumn equinox, which marks the harvest and the completion of the vegetation cycle of the year, as the days begin to grow colder and the light declines. It is the time of fullness and maturity.

Magically water rules emotions and feelings, including love and hate, daring and cowardice, happiness and sorrow, giving and taking. It also rules the intuition and psychic skills. Water is cleansing and purifying. It is the power of experience.

The most famous legend of a cup is that of the Holy Grail, the cup of enlightenment and drinking from it brings about union with the Divine. It has many antecedents, including the magical cauldrons of the Celts, but in Christian lore it takes the form of the chalice used at the Last Supper, which according to legend was brought to Britain by Joseph of Arimathea. In lore the knights of King Arthur searched for the mysterious Grail, which would heal the sacred king of his wound and make whole the land. The quest of each knight was personal and individual, subjecting them to many tests and challenges to prove themselves worthy, loyal and pure in heart and most fell by the wayside. The ritual cup can represent the Holy Grail of spiritual fulfilment which we all seek in our individual spiritual quests.

Legend has it that during the time of the persecutions, no special magical equipment was marked or set aside in any way, lest a search reveal it. The cup used in a Craft ceremony was simply the best cup in the house. Nor was the cup marked in any way outwardly, but rather consecrated with the sign of the pentagram drawn upon it in charged water and thus sacred to the Lord and Lady from that time forth. Today the cup is usually of silver, wood or clay. It is not bought but always given with love.

Consecrating a Cup

The cup is consecrated with incense of dragon's blood, blackberry, bindweed, primrose or red poppy and the following words:

> "*God and Goddess, deign to bless this cup which I would consecrate and set aside. Let it obtain the necessary virtues for acts of beauty and love in the names of the Lord and Lady.*" pass through the elements "*God and Goddess, I call upon you to bless this instrument which I have prepared in your honour.* "Hold it high in the air and say "*Let blessing be*". Use the new tool as soon as possible.

THE CAULDRON

A cauldron is essentially a cooking pot, a vessel which transforms the raw ingredients of life into something new. There are many cauldrons in Celtic myth, owned by various gods and goddesses. Some mysteriously produce sustenance, some transform, some hold the fruits of the harvest or give life. In essence all these cauldrons represent the transformative womb of the Goddess, which may be the vault of the heavens or the underground earth, in which seeds germinate and growth, and return to in death to grow once more- the cycle of all life.

Perhaps the most famous story of a cauldron concerns the Goddess Ceridwen who brewed a potion which contained all the wisdom of the Three Realms. The cauldron simmered for a year and a day. A little boy, Gwion, was given the job of feeding the fire beneath it. One day three drops fell from the cauldron onto his finger, which he put into his mouth to ease the pain. Instantly he was at one with all things, past, present and future. Furious that he had stolen the magic, Ceridwen pursued him in the form of a black hag. Gwion, using his new powers, changed himself into a hare but Ceridwen turned into a greyhound to catch him. Gwion jumped into a river and became a fish while Ceridwen proceeded to change herself into an otter and swam after him. He then flew from the river as a bird and Ceridwen became a hunting hawk. Hoping to elude her Gwion transformed himself into a grain of wheat on the threshing floor of a granary, but the goddess, becoming a black hen, ate him. For nine month Gwion remained in the womb of the goddess, until at last he was reborn as a beautiful boy child.

The story of Gwion relates the events of an initiation. First of all he stokes the cauldron of knowledge, then, when he least expects it, his consciousness is transformed. This all embracing knowledge then makes him afraid and he tries to run away from it. The goddess challenges him by assuming a frightening form to test his worthiness. He goes through different personifications of animal totems, assimilating the knowledge of different realities, while the confrontation of the goddess forces him on, refining his being. Eventually he has to be reassumed into the womb of the goddess in order to be reborn as a true initiate, one of the Twice Born.

Therefore the cauldron is a symbol of initiation, renewal, rebirth and plenty. It may contain water, fire, incense or flowers as the occasion demands. Leaping over the cauldron, like leaping over the broomstick, is a fertility rite.

Consecrating a Cauldron

The cauldron is consecrated with an incense of chervil and primrose with the following worlds:

> "*God and Goddess, deign to bless this cauldron which I would consecrate and set aside. Let it obtain the necessary virtues for acts of beauty and love in the names of the Lord and Lady.*" pass through the elements "G*od and Goddess, I call upon you to bless this instrument which I have prepared in your honour.*" Hold it and say "*Let blessing be*". Use the new tool as soon as possible.

THE WAND

The wand represents the fertilising phallus, which joins two opposites to transmit and create life, thus on a deeper level, the tool which joins the physical and the spiritual realms and transmits energy from one to the other. The wand relates to element of fire, the season of summer, noonday and the direction of the south. Its station on the wheel is the midsummer solstice, which we call Coamhain, when the earth flowers and grows lush. In the Celtic tradition the wand comes from the magical city of the south, Finias.

Magically, fire rules creativity, life energy and the spirit. Fire is the illumination within, the force of the spirit. Fire is the power of inner sight and creative vision, with strength of will directing it and controlling it to make it manifest in the world.

The function of the wand largely depends of which wood it is made from. For example an ash wand connects with the Sky God and invokes the cosmic axis, an apple wand, depending on when it is cut, may connect to the Summer Goddess and her gifts of love and fertility, or to Samhain and the Underworld with its secrets of transformation. A bay wand is connected with the sun and its power of healing, while rowan connects to the Goddess Brighid and rites of divination.

In ancient times when the races of the earth were pastoral, the patriarch bore his shepherd's crook and this crook, or wand, developed into the insignia of royalty, known as the sceptre. The rod was also the emblem of discipline and many ancient sculptures show the ruler wielding the rod over his subjects and captives. The rods of Moses and Aaron were considered to have been the original crosier of bishops. Classical mythology tells how Prometheus brought fire from heaven in a hollow wand.

Making a Wand

You should cut your own wand from living wood (see the instructions for cutting a staff). The time the wand is cut depends on what you want to use it for, but if you wanted to cut an oak wand, for example, you should go out before dawn on Midsummer Day and seek your chosen tree as the sun rises. The wood should be virgin, that is of one year's growth only, and the wand should be cut from the tree at a single stroke. It should measure from elbow to fingertip. Make a small hollow in the end that you will hold in your hand and insert of piece of cotton thread with a drop of your own blood into it, before sealing it with wax.

Consecrating a Wand

The wand is consecrated with an incense of bay, alder, birch, cedar, frankincense, hazel, sweet cicely or pine with the following words:

> "*God and Goddess, deign to bless this wand which I would consecrate and set aside. Let it obtain the necessary virtues for acts of beauty and love in the names of the Lord and Lady.*" Pass it through the elements in the following manner- push the tip into the earth, through the candle flame, into the dish of water and through the air in the sign of the pentacle, then say "*God and Goddess, I call upon you to bless this instrument which I have prepared in your honour.*" Hold it high in the air and say "*Let blessing be.*"

THE STAFF

It is no coincidence that wizards and shamans everywhere are depicted with a staff, though its purpose is very rarely understood -it is not a fancy walking stick or an accessory to make the magician look more imposing. The staff is a portable world tree or cosmic axis, which connects the magician to the three magical realms of the heavens, middle earth and the underworld. The World Tree grows with its roots in the underworld, its trunk in middle earth and its branches in the heavens, and connects all three. Therefore the staff is usually made of ash wood or some other symbolic World Tree wood, such as oak or apple.

Making a Staff

A staff should be a wooden pole the same height that you are and wide enough for your hand to curl comfortably around it. If you wish it may be carved with your personal symbols, but should not have any crystals incorporated into it.

The wood is taken from the living tree to capture the spirit of the tree is the subject of much misunderstanding. Some say that the wood must be taken in such a way as to capture the dryad of the tree, but this is a kind of shorthand for something much more profound. Every plant has its own spirit, which embodies its character, its magical vibration, its lessons and its complex connection within the Web of Being. Plants and trees must be approaches as individuals, and respected as living, spiritual entities. No two ash trees have the same personality, no two flax plants have the same qualities. To capture this is a difficult business, it is not simple a matter of walking three times around a tree and saying "can I have a branch?", lopping one off and leaving a coin in return (what the tree is supposed to do with this is anybody's guess). How many people know when they have got an answer? Is the plant even listening? You might as well buy a dried herb off the shelf in the local store, or pick up a dead twig from the garden. These instructions are based on folk magic, a distorted version of half forgotten lore, a shadow of the true knowledge.

First a relationship must be established with the particular tree you want to cut over a period of time; you must understand each other. Some trees are well disposed towards mankind, some need to be persuaded, some fought and some will never give you anything no matter what you do, and it would be dangerous to try. A staff may be consecrated with an incense of dragon's blood, flax, ash, birch, borage, sweet cicely, blackthorn or one of its other plant familiars according to how the staff is to be used.

THE ATHAME

Today there is much talk of swords, black handled knives (called athames) which are purely ritual in function and white handled knives (called curfanes or bollines) which are used to cut anything which needs cutting. These are concepts that have entered into the Craft from ritual magick. At one time a simple knife would be used for all purposes. In modern times the knife is a tool set aside and is usually consecrated at the time of initiation. It is usually used to cast the circle and invoke the cosmic axis and the quarters.

The knife corresponds to the element of air, the season of spring, the dawn and the direction of the east. Its station on the wheel is the spring equinox, which we call Ostara, when new life germinates and emerges with the increase of life and warmth. Magically, air rules all mental activity, from the inception of an idea to abstract knowledge, to the questioning of established theories.

In previous ages the forging of metal was a ritual act and the blacksmith was considered to be a magician, taking the raw materials from the underworld womb of Mother Earth and transforming them with air, fire and water. The shaping of metal equates to shaping the flow of life, which has potential for any form, and therefore to shaping destiny.

Making a Knife

In ceremonial magic and Wicca, the athame is made from iron or steel. In Wicce we use copper, silver or bronze since we wish to work with the spirits, not control them or frighten them away. While forging a blade is not possible for most, you can carve your own handle.

The kind of wood you use is up to you; you might want to choose something that you feel suitable after reading about the significance of the various woods. Soft woods often splinter with carving, while hard woods require sharper tools and more effort, but give a better result.

Take the block of wood and roughly sketch on it the shape of the handle you want to carve. Remove the bulk of the unwanted wood with a saw. Fix your work in a clamp and, taking a large gouging tool and mallet, gradually chip away small parts of the wood, working away from you, cutting with the grain. Keep working around the shape evenly, turning it as you need until you get the desired rough shape. Then using flat chisel begin rounding the handle. You also will need to carve a channel inside the handle to take the prong of the blade. When you have the shape smooth it with a rasp, then rub with coarse sandpaper, finally finishing it off with fine glass paper.

Heat equal amounts of beeswax and turpentine over a double boiler and paint it over the handle. When dry rub over with a soft cloth to polish.

Consecrating a Knife or Sword

The knife or sword is consecrated with an incense or oil of nettle, dragons blood or hellebore with the following words:

"I *conjure thee, O sword (or knife), that thou shall serve me as a strength and a defence in every magical ceremony. You shall defend me against my enemies, both visible and invisible. In the name of (god) and (goddess).*" Pass the sword through water and incense and the air in the sign of the pentacle and place on the earth. "'*I conjure thee O creature of steel, by the God and the Goddess whom we worship, by the waters and the wind, by earth and fire, that in your virtue I shall attain my desire, by the power of (god) and (goddess).*"

The Herb Knife

Herbs are never cut with iron or steel, as this earths the power of the plant. We all know that druids used golden sickles to represent both the power of the sun (the gold) and the power of the moon (the crescent shape) but not many of us could afford such an implement. Herb knives are usually made of copper or silver. The herb knife is consecrated with an incense, oil or tisane of centaury, the patron plant of herbalists.

Sword

The sword shares all the symbolism of the athame. It relates to the magical sword brought from the mystical city of Gorias, which no eye has seen but the soul knows. It appears in various guises as the most famously as Excalibur, the sword of Arthur. The sword is consecrated with an incense or oil of frankincense, nettle, dragons blood or hellebore.

THE PENTACLE

A copper, clay or stone disc marked with the sign of the pentagram is used as the elemental tool of the north. It relates to a much older symbol which is the stone or sometimes the shield or the mirror. In Celtic myth the Lia Fal is the stone of destiny, truth and wisdom which the Tuatha de Dannan brought from the Otherworld city of Falias ('truth').

The pentagram has become the accepted symbol of Paganism, first used in modern times by witches, but now also by Druids, Heathens and other Pagans. The word pentagram comes from the Greek *pentagrammon* meaning roughly 'five-lined'. It is the simplest form of star shape that can be drawn with a single line and therefore it is sometimes called the Endless Knot, but also known as the witch's foot, the Druid's foot and many other names.

The number five relates to the microcosm within the macrocosm. We humans have five sense, five fingers on each hand and five toes on each foot. We have five stages in out lives- birth, youth, adulthood, decline and death. Five-fold constructions frequently appear in life forms, but rarely in inanimate objects, so it is a symbol of life. The apple cut in half crossways reveals a pentacle in the centre.

The Roma refer to the core as the Star of Knowledge.

Its use in symbolism and magic dates back to at least 8000 years. In 3000 BCE it was used, two points up, in Sumerian pictograms which represent the word *UB* meaning a cavity or hole.

The pentagram is often said to be a symbol of the Goddess. It is particularly associated with Queens of Heaven and the planet Venus, since when viewed from the Earth, successive inferior conjunctions of Venus plot a nearly perfect pentagram shape around the zodiac every eight years.

In ancient Greece, the pentagram was a many-layered symbol for the Pythagoreans who considered it an emblem of perfection or the symbol of the human being. They called it the pentalpha, since it could be composed of five interlaced alphas (the Greek letter A) and *Hugieia*, meaning 'health', 'wholeness' or 'blessing', using the pentagram and the password *Hugiaine* ('Be Whole' or 'Be Blessed') and their secret sign and password after the school was suppressed. Hugieia (Hygeia) is the goddess of health, equivalent to the Roman Salus. The Pythagoreans labelled the points of the pentagram, with the Greek letters U, G, I, EI, A. It was depicted two points up, like the Babylonian pentagram, and may have had a similar meaning relating to the *Pentemychos* (a work written by Pythagoras' teacher and friend Pherecydes [1]) the 'five chambers' in the underworld were the five pre-cosmic offspring, representing disorder, had to be confined by Kronos (ordered time) so that the kosmos (the ordered world) could be born from Tartaros, the primordial darkness or Chaos.

Traditionally, the five elements of the ancients are attributed to the points of the pentacle, placed in the order of density - aether, fire, air, water, earth:

Earth: (lower left hand corner) represents stability and physical endurance.
Fire: (lower right hand corner) represents courage and daring.
Water: (upper right hand corner) represents emotions and intuition.
Air: (upper left hand corner) represents intelligence and the arts.
Spirit: (at the topmost point) represents the All and the Divine.

Though the modern Christian Church generally sees the pentacle as a symbol of the occult and evil, it has a long history of use within monotheistic traditions. During the times of the Old Testament, the pentacle was the first and most important of the Seven Seals, amulets which represent the seven secret names of God. The points of the pentagram also refer to the the five books of the Pentateuch - the first five books of the Torah. For Christians, the pentacle represented the five wounds of Christ and the star of Bethlehem, used as an amulet of protection.

---

1 Guardians of Darkness, Comrade August and Tani Jantsang, http://www.geocities.com/go_darkness/god-pythagorean-pentacle.html

In the Arthurian tales, Sir Gawain had a shield bearing the pentagram in gold on a red background. Its five points symbolise the five knightly values of generosity, courtesy, chastity, chivalry and piety.

With the development of the Hermetic arts in the Renaissance, and its interest in sacred geometry, the pentagram was used as the 'Star of the Microcosm', symbolising man (think of da Vinci's depiction of a man with arms and legs outstretched within a pentagram) and his relationship to the macrocosm. Similar contemporary images show the elements or planets arranged around the points of the pentagram.

As we have seen, the ancients often drew the pentacle with two points upwards, what we now call an inverted pentacle, which Hollywood and the popular media coupled with Satanism. The association seems to have begun in the nineteenth century with Eliphas Levi who illustrated the upright pentagram of microcosmic man beside an inverted pentagram containing the goat's head of Baphomet, which the literally minded took to be good and evil. Indeed, some modern day Satanists have adopted this sigil drawn within a double circle, replacing the Pythagorean letters with Hebrew ones spelling out 'Leviathan'. Crowley used the inverted pentagram to represent the descent of spirit into matter, as opposed to its ancient meaning of order emerging from chaos.

The pentagram is often depicted within a circle. The circle can be seen as representing infinity and eternity, the cycles of life, protection, the containment of the magic circle and its secrets, or the God and Goddess.

Most modern Pagans follow the Golden Dawn system, in which the pentacle is associated with the earth, and is one of the four magical tools of the adept. The disc corresponds to the element of earth, the season of winter, midnight and the direction of the North. Its station on the wheel is the midwinter solstice, which we call Yule, the time of chaos when the sun is reborn at the dead time of the year when the earth sleeps. From this point on the days begin to lengthen once more and though the worst of the winter weather is still to come, we have the promise of the return of spring.

Magically, the earth rules the body and the material plane. Earth is solid, the manifest world which supports and nourishes us. In token of this, bread is placed on the disc during the ritual, which is then blessed and shared before its close.

While it would be difficult for most people to gain access to the equipment to make a copper disc, a simple an effective pentacle can be made from rolled out clay, cut into a nine inch or twelve inch circle and inscribed with a pentagram and symbols which represent the earth to you. This should then be fired and glazed. A variety of modelling clays can be obtained from art shops that need no firing. An effective disc can be made from a sheet of slate. This does not have to be round, and can easily be incised with a sharp tool with suitable symbols. These can then be filled with gold paint. Similarly you could use a flat sheet of rock, but if it is of a hard variety the symbols will have to be painted on.

The pentacle may be consecrated with an oil, incense or infusion of clover in the usual manner.

Chapter 7
SEASONAL RITES

The Wheel of the Year concerns the flow of energy, pouring in at one part of the year and ebbing out at another. Our ancestors recognised this as a balance – a time to receive, a time to pay out. This is something not well understood nowadays when dark, death, winter are seen to be evil, rather than part of the Cosmic balance. For the Pagan death was not the end but part of the cycle: corn is sown, grows, is cut down and the seed re-sown to grow again in its season, a cycle we call the Eternal Return. The task of the Pagan is to understand this many layered pattern and work in harmony with, rather than in spite of, natural cycles.

The sun marks four clear divisions of the year at the two solstices and two equinoxes, which are referred to as the Quarter Days, and symbolised by the equal armed solar cross found widely depicted on pre-historical artefacts, and these are the oldest festivals of all. At the spring and autumn equinoxes, day and night are of equal length. At the summer solstice we have the longest day, and at the winter solstice, the longest night. These days have been observed by virtually every culture at some point in their histories. Into the modern neo-Pagan calendar are inserted the Cross Quarter Days to make eight festivals. These Cross Quarter festivals are also ancient, and were almost equally celebrated. They are based on the position of the stars rather than the sun, though today they are rarely celebrated on the true date which has moved with the precession of the equinoxes, but meshed with the fixed calendar. The fixed calendar moves us further from the original date by virtue of the fact that in 1582 Pope Gregory XIII wiped out ten days from the old Julian calendar to re-align it with the seasons. However, the Gregorian calendar was not adopted in Britain until 1752 and Ireland until 1782, by which time eleven days had to be dropped. This led to the festivals being celebrated on either the old date or the new, called respectively New Style and Old Style. As a general rule, most celebrations gradually moved to the New Style calendar.

There are no greater and lesser Sabbats, but each festival carries equal weight within the story of the year.

NB: The rituals in this book are suggestions, sketches of rituals, some with invocations and some without. It is u to you to flesh them out and adapt them to your needs, or simply take some of the ideas and formulate your own.

YULE

The winter solstice was celebrated on every continent of the earth; by the ancient Egyptians, Babylonians, Jews, Persians, Greeks, Roman, Norse, Celtic and Germanic, in North and South America, the Far and Near East and Africa.

The winter solstice takes place on or about December 21st every year in the northern hemisphere (or 21st June in the southern hemisphere). The sun hangs low and weak in the sky during the brief daylight hours, casting long shadows. It is the shortest day and longest night, but from this time the sun gradually strengthens; thus it is the death of the old solar year and the start of the new.

Ancient man would have realised that we depend on the sun for life- in the summer the long hours of daylight and warmth make the crops grow. In the winter days of darkness and cold, they shrivel and die; humans and animals struggle to find food and survive. Each day, up to the winter solstice, the sun grows weaker and weaker. If it does not regenerate then life must end. Then, on the shortest day in the time of darkness, the light is reborn and with it hope.

'Solstice' is derived from two Latin words: sol meaning 'sun', and sistere, 'to cause to stand still' and so means 'sun stands still'. A little before and during the winter and summer solstices, the sun appears to rise and set at almost exactly the same place on the horizon. Throughout the year the sun passes through the constellations of the zodiac and the summer solstice occurs in the constellation of Cancer, the Crab, and the winter solstice in the constellation of Capricorn, the Goat. At the moment of the winter solstice, the path of the sun in the sky over the past six months has reached its furthest southern position and now turns northward again.

The winter solstice is generally considered to be the start of winter, and the three winter months are reckoned as December, January and February. However, the 'solar winter'- the period with the fewest hours of daylight and the weakest sunlight - stretches from November 1st to February 1st with the solstice marking Midwinter.

Though the Winter Solstice is the shortest day of the year, it is not the date of either the earliest sunset or the latest sunrise. The earliest sunset occurs around Little Yule on 13th December, and the latest sunrise around New Year at the beginning of January.

The celebration of the winter solstice dates back at least 10,000 years and possibly very much earlier. Many archaic structures, such as stone circles and the burial chambers, have winter solstice alignments. Stonehenge is not only orientated to the summer sunrise as many think, but also to the winter solstice sunrise and sunset along the main axis of the temple. The temples of Karnak and Abydos (in Egypt) have winter solstice alignments and the Sun Dagger celestial calendar in New Mexico offers a direct alignment with both the winter solstice sunset and summer solstice sunrise. Newgrange in Ireland was designed to funnel a shaft of sunlight deep into its central chamber at dawn on the day of the Winter Solstice. Above the entrance way is a stone box that allows the light from the sun to penetrate to the back of the cairn at sunrise. Its older name was *An Liamh Greine* or 'the Cave of the Sun'.

It was a common belief that the sun spent each night or each winter in a cave. Many solar deities are said to have been born from a cave: Mithras dragged the solar bull from a cave; Zeus was born in the Dictean Caves on Crete; the god Krishna was born in a dark dungeon; Apollo was born under Delos, where no rays of sunlight could penetrate; the Phoenician god Melkarth woke from his winter sleep in his sacred cave at the winter solstice and the Japanese sun goddess Amaterasu lived in a cave for a time. In early Christian stories, Jesus was born in a cave - the Greek text of the Gospel of St Luke uses the word *katalemna*, meaning cave, not stable - and in Bethlehem the Church of the Nativity is built over a cave.

The sun god is always said to be the son of a virgin- he is born at the winter solstice at midnight when the sign of Virgo the Virgin is rising above the horizon. In ancient Egypt the incarnated god and saviour Osiris died and was entombed at the winter solstice, then at midnight, the priests emerged from an inner shrine crying *"The Virgin has brought forth! The light is waxing"* and showing the image of a baby to the worshipers, the infant Horus, Osiris reincarnated. The festival lasted twelve days (the origin of the twelve days of Christmas) to reflect the twelve months of the year.

It was a common belief that the twelve days of Yule were connected to the twelve months ahead. In Britain, the weather on each day reflected that which could be expected in the corresponding month. In Germany and Scandinavia, the twelve months of the year are magically reflected during the twelve holy nights when the Wild Hunt rides out. It is an especially dangerous time when spirits are abroad.

The legendary King Arthur ('Bear-Man') was identified with the constellation of the Great Bear which was called Arthur's Wain (wagon), or sometimes Arthur's Plough. The bear hibernates in the winter, entering a cave or some quiet, secluded place. It emerges in the spring with the female often having given birth in the meantime and appearing with cubs in tow. This led to the bear being associated with regeneration and rebirth, adopted as a solar symbol. It seems likely that Arthur was originally a sun/bear god, with the solstice being called *Alban Arthur* or 'Arthur's Time' by modern Druids. Arthur's marriage to the Earth causes it to blossom. During the year he is a warrior who battles the darkness. In the winter he is the aging sun king who dies, sleeping in a cave until his promised return.[aw] Following the Great Bear is the constellation of Boötes, the herdsman, with its brightest star Arcturus or 'Bear Keeper'. When it first rises over the eastern horizon, not long after the winter solstice each year, it means that spring is on its way. Arcturus is known as 'The One who Comes', and just as Arthur is known as the 'Once and Future King.' The constellation of the Great Bear circles around the still Pole Star during the course of the year. To this day the Welsh refer to the northern heavens as the Bwrdd Arthur (Arthur's Table), described as round. [ax]

For the Romans, Dies Natalis Invicti Solis, 'the Birthday of the Unconquered Sun' celebrated the birth of Sol (the sun). Roman women would parade in the streets crying *"unto us a child is born!"* In the old Julian calendar the winter solstice, or Bruma 'the shortest day,' fell on December 25th.

The Romans also held the Saturnalia festival at the winter solstice, and it is the origin of many Yuletide customs we still enjoy today. Saturn (from *satus* meaning 'sowing'). Cognate with the Greek Kronos, is one of the elder Roman deities, a god of time and agriculture. The feast commemorated the mythical age of Saturn's kingship, a Golden Age of happiness for all men. Like Arthur, it is said that he lies asleep on a secret island and one day will return. In the meantime, once a year a temporary Golden Age was celebrated. Riotous merry-making took place, and lights were kept burning to ward off the spirits of darkness. Schools were closed, the army rested, and no criminals were executed. Friends visited one another with gifts of cakes, lamps, dolls, jewellery and incense. Temples were decorated with evergreens symbolizing life's continuity, and processions of people with masked or blackened faces danced through the streets. Masters served meals to their slaves who elected a Mock King to take charge of the revels. This custom continued with the Mediaeval Lord of Misrule who presided over the Christmas festivities.

There is an element of anarchy and the reversal of social order about the Yuletide festivities, because the dying of the sun threatens a descent into primal chaos: it the end of the old cycle of existence, and order is restored only with its rebirth. The intervening period or 'gap in time,' the inter-calendar days of the twelve days of Yule, is especially magical and otherworldly, being a time on the verge of chaos when the barriers between the realms dissolve, when the veils between the living and dead are thin. Finnish shamans call it 'The Dreaming' or 'God's Trance Hour'.[ay] Several fairies are said to destroy any spinning left on the wheel at Yule or Christmas. This has its origin in the fact that many sun gods and goddesses were associated with spinning, either spinning the Cosmos itself, or sunbeams in the hours before dawn. At Yule, the midwinter solstice, when the sun stands still, all forms of spinning and weaving were forbidden because it was a pause in the turning of the wheel of the year. The Lapps forbade the turning of any kind of wheel, including cartwheels and churns.

Stories surrounding the winter solstice often tell of a battle between light and dark, during which the light triumphs. The battle of the summer and winter king at Augsburg, where summer wears ivy and evergreens and winter is masked, is marked by a fight between the two in which summer wins. In Steiermark winter and summer are teams of young men. The winter men wear fur jackets and have baker's shovels, flails and reels of twine. The summer men have sickles, scythes and pitchforks.

All of the customs associated with the modern Christmas are Pagan in origin. A December festival to celebrate the birth of Christ didn't exist until the fourth century when Christians simply adopted the popular solstice celebrations honouring the birth of the divine child, the sun. The eastern churches refused to honour it for another hundred years, and the church of Jerusalem ignored the date until the 7th century. John Chrysostom, a fourth-century bishop of Constantinople firmly believed December 25th was selected so Christians could celebrate Christ's birthday undisturbed while "*the heathen were busy with their profane ceremonies*".[az]

Fire is the little brother of the sun, so fires were lit at the solstice to encourage (by sympathetic magic) the sun to strengthen and begin the long climb back to midsummer. Around the fire would dance shamans dressed in deer skins and antlers, goat hide and horse head skulls and masks. Red was worn to give strength to the sun.

To keep alive the vegetation spirit houses were decorated with evergreens, holly, ivy and mistletoe. Evergreens had great power as they could withstand the winter death. The mistletoe grows not on the ground, but on the branches of a tree, so it was considered very magical. The berries were regarded as the semen of the host tree, or by some the semen of the Lord of the Trees. The most sacred mistletoe grew on the oak (a rare occurrence). The mistletoe represented the vitality of the oak and was used to strengthen the sun god in his weakened state. Amongst the Celts, warfare had to cease at the time of the winter solstice and mistletoe cutting. Later, Christian cathedrals and churches would lay mistletoe on the altar for the Twelve Days of Christmas and in some cities, such as York, a general pardon would be proclaimed at the gates.

In Scandinavian and other northern countries, including some Celtic ones, evergreen trees were decked with lights. The Romans decorated pine trees with images of Bacchus (Dionysus).

The custom of holly decoration was carried on into the Christian era although it was not to be brought in until Christmas Eve or allowed to remain after Twelfth Night. The ivy is a symbol of life and rebirth as it remains green throughout the winter and for its spiral growth, which represents the path of the sun (as do the spiral patterns at Newgrange).

Father Christmas is one of a number of gift-giving spirits that appear at the winter solstice, depending on which country you live in. It is possible that he evolved from the Scandinavian/Germanic god Odin or Woden, who rode the skies at Yule wearing a red, bloody, flayed animal skin, punishing the wicked and rewarding the good. It seems likely that he passed into English folklore and can be traced in the character that appears as master of ceremonies in the mumming plays, and as the King of Christmas. Perhaps the figure may be older still, originating in the Druidic midwinter festivities and the Roman Saturnalia or the tribal shaman dressed in red and white to echo the fly agaric mushroom. In European legends he rides a goat or a donkey, the latter a Saturnalian beast sacrificed with a holly club at the midwinter solstice. In Germany, he is also known as Pelze Nicol ('Furry Nicholas' from his fur costume), who is titled *Schrimmerlreiter* 'Rider of the White Horse,' one of the titles of Odin.

THEMES OF YULE

- Rebirth of light, renewal, regeneration
- The Child of Promise
- Hope in the time of greatest darkness
- Encouraging the sun with fire, light, sun-shaped decorations on the tree
- Evergreen life persisting in the time of death
- Order rescued from chaos
- Death of the old, birth of the new
- A time apart, a pause, a breath before the cycle continues
- Cessation of hostilities, peace and goodwill
- The levelling of social barriers, a reversal of social order
- Reward and punishment for the deeds of the year- a time of reckoning
- What rebirth do you seek?
- What ending do you seek, what do you need to leave behind?

SAMPLE RITE FOR YULE

Cast the circle in the usual manner. The God and Goddess are invoked.

Priest: I*n this the season of the Dark Time, shrouded in the frosted cloak of the Crone, we celebrate the festival of Yule, the rebirth of the sun, and the life of the coming year.*

Priestess:
In the coldness of winter we hunger
In the stillness of winter we are silent
In the ice of winter we are caught in the north wind's blast
In the depths of winter the world is wrapped in sleep

We need the fire in our hearts to love
We need the fire in the hearth to eat
We need the fire in the head to make
We need the fire in the heavens to live

Priest: *The year has reached its lowest ebb, all is darkness and death. Yet in this darkness we must find hope. In this darkness we must find light. The sun must be reborn!*

He then leads the dance and chant which everyone joins in:
Water, air, fire and earth
Bring the Sun God to rebirth

Each person takes a token, usually the remains of last year's mistletoe, or an object that symbolises something you wish to be rid of, or a piece of paper on which you have written all the things you wish to be rid of (such as bad habits, illness, old ties, destructive relationships and so on) and invokes into it all that they wish to leave behind with the passing year. This is then burned in the fire.

Bard:
At the threshold of the Underworld, the Dark God waits,
As death moves to life and dark turns to light
The Lord of the Dead, he stalks the land,
The Bringer of Chaos, he stalks the land,
The Keeper of Mysteries, he stalks the land.
The year ebbs and the wheel spins as
Dark turns to light
At the threshold of the Underworld, the Dark God waits.

Through the underworld the God has passed
Open the gate and let him in.

At the threshold of the year, the Stag Lord waits,
Hunter and the hunted; red blood on white snow,
Antlered God of winter stillness, waiting
Our sacrifice of flesh for life, waiting
On the edge of the forest, the Lord is waiting,
He knows the ancient secret of
Red blood on white snow,
At the threshold of the year, the Stag Lord waits.

Through the underworld the God has passed
Open the gate and let him in.

At the threshold of life, the Green Man waits,
Ivy clad, scarlet berries, dark green leaves,

Ever green and ever growing, pauses,
The moment nears and yet he pauses,
The light will come, till then he pauses,
In the holly and the ivy,
Scarlet berries, dark green leaves,
At the threshold of life, the Green Man waits.

Our God has passed through the underworld
Open the gate and let him in.

On the threshold of dawn, the Sun King waits,
The light of the world, gold light in black sky.
On the rim of the world, the Sun King dances,
Our child of promise, the Sun King dances,
At his moment of birth, the Sun King dances,
The light of our hope,
Gold light in black sky.
On the threshold of dawn, the Sun King waits.

Our God has passed through the underworld
Open the gate and let him in.

Queen of Heaven and Queen of Earth
Queen of death and Queen of birth
Queen of sadness, grieving, bane
Grant our God returns again,
Grieving wife and widowed Mother
Awaken now thy son, thy lover.
Give him birth from womb of night
Renew the world with the power of light.
Give to us the promised One
The shining, radiant, beautiful Sun.

On the threshold of dawn, the Sun King waits,
The light of the world, gold light in black sky.
On the rim of the world, the Sun King dances,
Our child of promise, the Sun King dances,
At his moment of birth, the Sun King dances,
The light of our hope,

Gold light in black sky.
On the threshold of dawn, the Sun King waits.

Our God has passed through the underworld
Open the gate and let him in.

Sun King: (wearing a sun mask lights candles around the circle.)"*The light is reborn!*"

Priest: "*With the sun we are each reborn. Blessed Be!*"

All : "*Blessed Be.*"

Meditation, magic etc is performed.
Bread and wine.
The circle is broken.

IMBOLC

Imbolc is the modern Pagan festival that marks the return of spring and life after the darkness and death of winter. It was one of the four pastoral festivals of our Celtic ancestors, but was also recognised and celebrated in other parts of the world under different names. It was finally Christianised as Candlemas, and some Pagans still call it by this name.

After Yule, light increases at the rate of two minutes a day, and by Imbolc, this increase is very conspicuous. The Earth can be seen responding to it, and begins to stir back into action. Snowdrops and crocuses flower and early trees begin to bud. Animals start to emerge from hibernation and lambing begins - an obvious sign of regeneration and renewal.

Various scholars have derived the word Imbolc from *Ol-melc* (ewe's milk) because the ewes are lactating at this time, or from *Im-bolg* (in the belly) implying the swelling belly of the Earth Goddess, or *folcaim* (I wash) because this is a time of purification.

We celebrate Imbolc as the time when the Hag of Winter is transformed into the Spring Goddess, renewed in her virginity. In ancient Rome young boys would play a game in which an old woman released a dragon (presumably representing winter) which must be fought and overcome, while a young maiden released a lamb. The winter hag Bera released Brigit in spring, according to the Scots.

The coming of Imbolc is inextricably linked to the ending of the winter season of rest and withdrawal. Very little work was done on the land from Samhain till Imbolc. It was also the time of the ploughing of the first furrow into which the corn dolly, kept safely in the farmhouse since the harvest, would be inserted to return fertility to the land. The ploughs were brought out, cleaned and blessed on Plough Monday (the first Monday after Twelfth Night) to make them ready for the wok ahead.

Though we now consider Twelfth Night to be the end of the Yuletide season, in the past many considered this was Candlemas. Like Twelfth Night, it was marked by games, dancing and feasting presided over by the Lord of Misrule or Abbot of Unreason. The Yule log was often burned up until Candlemas Eve. The custom prevailed in some parts of Britain until the early twentieth century. Even now in Rome, the manger scenes are left up until Candlemas. In England, it was the time to take down the Yuletide decorations.

At this time of year, following the Great Bear is the constellation of Bootes, the herdsman. When its Brightest star Arcturus or 'Bear Keeper', first rises over the eastern horizon in January, it means that spring is on its way. The Celtic Goddess Brighid was styled 'daughter of the bear', as her early spring festival of Imbolc follows the rising of Arcturus.

Brighid is pan-Celtic goddess, appearing as Brighid or Brigit in Ireland, Brigantia in Northern England, Bride in Scotland, and Brigandu in Brittany. Her name is variously interpreted as deriving from *breo-saighead* "Fiery Arrow" or "The Bright One", or from the root Sanskrit word *Brahti* meaning "The Powerful One" or "The High One". She was originally a sun and fire goddess, born at sunrise on threshold of the house as her mother was on her way out to milk the cow, and immediately a tower of flame emerged from her forehead that stretched from earth to heaven. She is a goddess of transformation: the transformation of ore to metal objects, seed to birth, inspiration to poetry and the passage from winter to spring.

Finding that the worship of the Pagan goddess Brighid was too deeply ingrained to be eradicated, the Christians turned her into a saint, St. Brigid, given the role as the nursemaid of Jesus, though she was supposed to have lived several centuries later in the 5th - 6th century CE, and to have founded an abbey in Kildare. In Christian myth she was the foster mother of Jesus who distracted Herod's soldiers by dancing with two candles, so that the holy family could escape. This is a direct appropriation of the role of the Pagan goddess nurturing the Child of Light, born at the winter solstice and growing stronger with each passing day, reflected in the increasing light. Her ancient festival became Candlemas when church candles were blessed.

The other direct ancestors of the Christian festival Candlemas and the modern Pagan Imbolc are the ancient Roman festivals of the Parentalia and Feralia, celebrations of purification in honour of the goddess Juno. On February 1st the

Romans celebrated the feast of Juno Sospita (Juno the Saviour). The consuls made a sacrifice to her, while young girls offered barley-cakes to the sacred snake in her grove. If their offerings were accepted, their virginity was confirmed and the year's fertility assured. The cave where offerings were made is in Lanuvio, about 40 km from Rome. The name Lanuvio is thought to be derived from "The goddess covered in wool (*lana*)" since this is the season when ewes give birth. The month of February is named after another aspect of Juno, Juno Februata or Juno the Fructifier, from *februare* meaning 'to expiate, to purify'. Priests ran about the city, scourging women with *februa* ('means of purification') which were strips of skin taken from a sacrificed goat. The Romans believed that this flogging would purify them and assure their future fertility and easy childbirth. In 494 CE, Pope Gelasius I tried to appropriate the festival by calling it the Feast of the Purification of the Virgin Mary to mark the time when Mary was purified in the temple after giving birth to Christ. This echoes the purification of seasonal goddesses, like Aphrodite, who bathe in pools to renew their virginity i.e. the earth washed clean by the spring rains.

THEMES OF IMBOLC

- Increasing light
- Hearth fire
- Creative fire
- Healing fire
- Women and the Goddess
- Purification
- Renewal of maidenhood
- Renewal of the land and wakening the earth
- Returning to work on the land after the winter lull
- Renewal of fertility with the birth of lambs and growth in plants
- How do you use the three fires of Brighid?

SAMPLE IMBOLC RITUAL

All the women prepare 'Brighid's Bed' to which the Goddess is invited to witness the proceedings. A soft pallet is prepared from straw, heather, rushes and rich blankets and set about with candles and lamps. Everyone prepares two garlands-one representing winter (made from old Yule decorations, dead winter twigs etc. and one representing spring made from green shoots, spring flowers etc. The winter garland is worn and the spring garland kept by.

The circle is cast by the women.

Priestess 1: "*Queen and Lady, Goddess of the Night. Secret Goddess, thy servants call upon thee, for this is the time of thy festival. Come now and enter our circle. Enter Lady, come now to thy bed and bless thy servants.*"

Priestess 2: *We are gathered here tonight to celebrate Imbolc, the festival of the Goddess and womankind. We ask the Goddess to rekindle life in the earth and bless us with her inspiration.*

Priestess 3: (Lighting the fire)*Let this fire in the centre of the circle represent the perpetual fire of the spirit of the Goddess. Let it be a beacon to call the Old Gods to us. The Lady's fire gives life to the strengthening sun, and to each of us.*

Priestess 1: (Throwing the winter garlands on the fire) T*he dead time is past, the wheel turns towards new life and spring.*

Priestess 2: *The rains of spring wash winter from the earth. They nurture the growing shoots of life as the ewe feeds the young lamb. They transform the Hag of Winter into the Maiden of Spring.*

Priestess 1: *The Goddess is every woman and every woman is the Goddess- let each of you wash in the cauldron, be purified in mind, body and spirit. Let the water transform you into a new Self, like the Maiden of Spring, ready to grow and flower with the year.* She washes in the cauldron and puts on her spring garland. Everyone washes in the cauldron, helped by the others, then puts on the spring garland.

Priestess 3 then washes the crystal in the water to symbolise the spring rains cleansing the earth and explains the symbolism as she does so.

Priestess 1: (Picks up the wand) *This is the white wand of the Goddess, the feminine power of fertility and inspiration. With this I breathe the life of spring into the mouth of dead winter.* She points the wand towards the earth, the sky and the four quarters.

Priestess 3: *Brighid's fire is the warmth and comfort of the hearth; it is the creative fire of the smith's forge; it is the inspirational fire in the head.*

After this each person states to the others what they have to offer to the Goddess in terms of their talents and strengths, what they have to offer the world and themselves. After this scry in the crystal, mirror or fire. When all is finished:

Priestess 1: (Takes up the cup of wine) "*The cup is the womb of the Goddess from which we are all born. It is the cauldron of transformation from which we are nurtured and fed. As we drink of this cup we share in these gifts of the Goddess.*" (All drink.)

Priestess 2: "*These cakes are from the body of the Mother Earth, who sustains our lives with her gifts. As we eat of them may we know of the love of the Goddess.*"

Priestess 3: *The Goddess has witnessed our rites and seen the truth of our hearts. Let this rite be ended in perfect love and perfect trust. Blessed Be.*

The circle is broken.

OSTARA

Ostara celebrates the vernal equinox when day and night stand at equal length (twelve hours each) but the light is gaining and the days are getting longer. We can really feel spring in the air, and notice the ever increasing warmth and the burgeoning of life. We experience a resurgence of vigour and hope as the energies of the natural world shift from the lethargy of winter to the lively expansion of spring.

After the bareness of winter, Imbolc has opened the year as Brighid brings light and energy to the world. At Ostara, the gods and goddesses of fertility return to the land, and we see new growth everywhere. The flowering of the gorse, daffodils, primrose and coltsfoot - sun coloured spring flowers - celebrate and reflect the increasing strength of the sun. Animals and birds are nest building and mating.

Two thousand years ago, across the world, there were a variety of Pagan religions with markedly similar themes of a god who dies and is reborn. It is a universal Pagan theme, and one still echoed in the Christian Church today with the crucified and resurrected Christ. Ancient Pagan festivals were concerned with the natural world – the movements of the sun, moon, stars and constellations (giving rise to the myths of solar and sky deities); the seasons and plant life (the vegetation gods) and the mysteries of life, fertility, death and rebirth. Consequently, there are two types of slain and risen deities, the sun god and the vegetation god.

The sun god is usually born in a cave or underground chamber on the winter solstice, grows with the year, declines, dies and is reborn at the winter solstice again. They have titles that include such names as the Light of the World, Light Bringer and Saviour, and dedicate their lives to the service of humankind. Eventually they are overcome by the powers of darkness, several have 'last suppers', die and descend into the underworld, only to rise again, bringing salvation to the world.

The vegetation deity emerges from a cave (or the underworld) at the spring equinox. He represents the vegetative cycles of the year: the grain grows and is cut down or sacrificed only to be reborn again; the trees lose their leaves and seem to die only to shoot once more. Both types of resurrection gods spend a period in the underworld as kings of the dead. The rebirth of both is seen as the spiritual and physical salvation of the world.

Dumuzi was the consort of the goddess Inanna called 'The Shepherd' who helped the sheepfolds to multiply, the farmer who made the fields fertile, and under his rule there was plentiful vegetation and grain. The young god Dumuzi courted the goddess Inanna. Their mating at the Spring Equinox caused the earth to blossom and fruit. Then the heat of high summer during the Dog Days dried up the grasslands and the milk within the cattle. The young god was dying; he was lamented and mourned as the Wild Bull who was sacrificed, who lay down and lived no more (the Bull of Heaven, Taurus, which disappears for six weeks from the Sumerian Horizon from January to March). As the grain was cut and stored or made into beer, the god was said to go into the underworld to return next year when the sap rose in the trees and vegetation returned to the earth. The Babylonian New Year was celebrated at the Spring Equinox, a twelve day celebration of renewal and the promise of fertility. The marriage of Dumuzi and Inanna bring life back to the earth, the renewal of the seasons, and their love transforms the world.

Adonis ('Lord') was worshipped by the Semitic peoples of Babylonia and Syria, and this worship spread to Greeks as early as the 7th century BCE. The legend is a variation of the Sumerian Tammuz story. In Syria, his lover goddess was called Astarte who was adopted by the Greeks as Aphrodite, the goddess of love. In the spring a festival of his resurrection was held; the women set out to seek him, and having found the supposed corpse (represented by a wooden image) placed it in a coffin or hollow tree, and performed wild rites and lamentations, followed by rejoicings over his resurrection.

The incarnated Greek god Dionysus was celebrated at the Spring Equinox, the Greater Dionysia, when vegetation is renewed.

In Phrygia the spring equinox marked the resurrection of Attis, a vegetation god and lover of the Great Goddess Cybele. In ancient Rome, the ten day festival in honour of Attis began on March 15th. A pine tree, which represented Attis, was chopped down, wrapped in a linen shroud, decorated with violets and placed in a sepulchre in the temple. On the 'Day of Blood' or 'Black Friday', the priests of the cult gashed themselves with knives as they danced ecstatically, sympathizing with Cybele in her grief and helping to restore Attis to life. Two days later, a priest opened the sepulchre at dawn, revealing that it was empty and announcing that the god was saved. This day was known as *Hilaria* or the Day of Joy, a time of feasting and merriment. In Rome, the rituals took place where St. Peter's now stands in Vatican City.

Mithras was worshipped widely among the Persians, Indians, Romans and Greeks up till around 400 CE. He was born in a cave of a virgin mother attended by shepherds, on December 25th and his religion spread with the Roman Empire and nearly took over the known world. He was the known as the 'Light of the World', 'The Redeemer' and 'The Good Shepherd'. He baptised his followers and shared a Last Supper. An inscription on the temple of Mithras which lies beneath the Vatican reads "*He who will not eat of my body, nor drink of my blood, so that he may be one with me and I with him, shall not be saved.*" He travelled far and wide as a teacher and had twelve companions. He was buried in a tomb, rose again at the spring equinox, which was celebrated with great rejoicing. He was sometimes figured as a lamb, and his sacred day was Sunday.

Easter is an annual Christian festival celebrating the resurrection of Jesus Christ after his willing sacrifice and crucifixion on Good Friday and his entombment for three days. It is held on the first Sunday after the first full moon after the Vernal Equinox. He seems to be a fusion of many earlier Pagan death and resurrection saviour gods, and Christianity an attempt to blend a variety of different ancient mystery regions, myths, and traditions into one. Indeed, when Paganism and Christianity overlapped, the rites of Attis and Jesus took place on the same date, with Pagans and Christians arguing over which was the original, and which the imitation, even though the rites of Attis had been celebrated in Rome two hundred and fifty years before the advent of Christianity.

This Christian holiday was named after a Saxon goddess of spring (Eostre) in the 8th century, but before that it was known as *Hebdonada Alba*, 'White Week', because of the white robes worn by the newly baptized. The Saxon hare-headed goddess of spring is Eostre or Ostara, the name derived from a root word meaning 'dawn'; from it we also get our word 'east', the station of the spring equinox as the sun rises in the east. The east and the hare are also associated with male deities, messengers and light bringers such as Thoth, Mercury and Hermes, as swell as slain and risen gods such as Osiris and Christ. The belief in the "Easter hare" bringing eggs was first recorded in German where children still build nests for the hare to lay its eggs in.

The hare is the most important Goddess totem at Ostara. For the Celts the hare was a sacred animal and there was a strict taboo on killing it. In Celtic countries, well into Victorian times, people would not eat the hare. The taboo was lifted at the equinox or Beltane and the hare was eaten to partake of its magical fertility. The Easter Hare Pie Scramble still takes place in Hallaton in Leicestershire.

Lamb was considered an essential part of the festival fare. Because the lamb is born in the month of purification, it is a representation of innocence and purity. This symbolism is widely used in the Christian religion, where Christ is 'the lamb without blemish', the suitable sacrifice. There is a superstition that the sun dances as it rises on Easter morning, and a lamb with a flag appears on it. At the spring equinox, around 21st March, the sun enters the constellation of Aries the Ram- Chrysomallon whose fleece was stolen by Jason and transported to the stars. Physical sheep are reported to bow three times to the east to welcome the rising sun. In Rome the spring equinox was the shepherd's festival, and a month later came the festival of the goddess Pales, patroness of shepherds.

Another essential Easter food was eggs. The laying capacity of hens is affected by light levels, and during the winter they lay very few eggs. With the coming of the equinox, they begin to produce again in earnest. Eggs were gathered (the origin of the Easter egg hunt) and used for the creation of talismans and also ritually eaten. The ancient Egyptians and Romans gave each other presents of eggs at the spring equinox as a symbol of resurrection and continuing life. The egg, dyed red, represented the resurrection of the sun. Christians adopted the egg as a symbol of the resurrected Christ. It was common to give children hard boiled eggs dyed red as the symbol of his blood. This would keep them healthy for the coming year. In England, there were also games based around dyed and painted eggs rolled down hillsides until they broke and were eaten. In this case the egg represents the passage of the sun.

The egg is a symbol of life and creation, and so of resurrection. In Hindu tradition the divine bird laid the cosmic egg on the primordial waters and from it sprang Brahma and the two halves formed heaven and earth. The cosmic tree is sometimes depicted as growing out of an egg floating on the waters of chaos. In Egyptian legend the Nile Goose laid the cosmic egg from which Ra, the sun, sprang. In China the yolk was the sky and the white the earth. The egg is closely associated with the serpent. One Egyptian legend says that Kneph, the serpent, produced the egg from his mouth. Orphism, holding the egg to be the mystery of life, creation and resurrection, often depicted the egg surrounded by Ouroboros, the circular serpent with its tail in its mouth. The Druids called the cosmic egg the egg of the serpent.

The egg is a prime symbol of Ostara and the rebirth of the year. We use it to represent that rebirth, and also our own inner rebirth at this time of year, when the weather warms and our horizons become expanded. From our winter introversion and keeping close to the hearth, we go out and accomplish things. It is time to put to work the lessons we have learned from our winter reflections and to bring that knowledge into the world. The egg reflects that potential, already once born, but waiting for its hatching. In the ritual the egg stands for our spiritual hopes in this yearly cycle.

THEMES OF OSTARA:

- The dancing sun, dawn
- The balance of light and darkness, the light gaining
- The Green man/ Vegetation God
- Renewal, life, vigour
- Fresh greenery, flowers
- Youth, virility, freshness
- Maiden Goddess, youthful God
- Eggs
- Hare, fertility, lambs, serpents

SAMPLE RITUAL FOR OSTARA:

The circle is cast and the Gods invoked.

Priestess: *We are gathered here tonight to celebrate the festival of Ostara, when the Lord and the Lady meet as youth and maid. It is the festival of spring, when all about us life renews. The sun strengthens, moving towards summer and his time of glory...*

Priest: holds up the sun wheel in the east and speaks about the dawn, the Ostara sun and the growing year in his own words.

Priestess: (Taking up the bowl of seeds) *The Goddess walks amongst us in all her maiden beauty. Come Lady, bless the seeds which shall become the flowers of Beltane and the harvest of Lughnasa. Bless the new born animals and the fledgling birds. We bless them in your name, O Goddess.*

Priest: *Our gentle Lord walks amongst us, clad in green. Come Lord, bless the seeds which shall become the flowers of Beltane and the harvest of Lughnasa. Bless the new born animals and the fledgling birds. We bless them in your name, O God.*

Priestess: *Let the seed be cast to the earth. Let the fire of joy be lit which is the light of the growing sun and the light of the year.*

The beacon is lit to symbolise the emergence of the year –and us- from darkness. The seeds are then gathered up and placed on one side to be divided up later amongst the celebrants.

Priest: Picks up the bowl of eggs and explains what they symbolise. The dish of eggs is then passed around and each person takes their egg and says what the egg means for them. It is then thrown through the circle in the direction that corresponds with those wishes (e.g. earth (north) for material desires, like a new job, fire (south) for spiritual desires, energy and so on, air (east) for study, water (west) for emotional/relationship matters).

Now is the moment for healing and magic of all kinds.
Meditation follows.
Bread and wine.
Break the circle.

BELTANE

In Ireland, the first of May was called *Bealtaine/ Beltene* (pronounced Bel-ti-na), with the modern Irish spelling of Beltane. The meaning of the word Beltane is not clearly understood. While *tene* means 'fire' it is not known whether Bel refers to the Celtic god of light Bel or *bel*, simply meaning 'brilliant'. It might even derive be *bil tene* or 'lucky fire' because people jumped between the two Beltane fires for luck. In Gaul there was a god called Belenos who Julius Caesar identified with the Greek/Roman sun god Apollo. In Britain Bel was a sun god, but in Ireland Bilé was the god of the underworld, the father of Miled. According to the ancient Irish 'Book of Invasions', the first settler of Ireland, Partholan, arrived on May 1st; and it was on May 1st that the plague came which destroyed his people. Years later, the Tuatha De Danann were conquered by the Milesians on May Day.

In Celtic tradition, the night of April 30th was thought of as the darkest of the year, when evil witches flew out to frighten people, and spirits roamed the land. People tried to frighten them off by banging kettles, doors and ringing bells. They kept a vigil through the night with blazing torches and fires to keep them off. In Bavaria it was called *Drudennacht* or 'Druid Night' when witches flew into the Harz Mountains and met at the Brocken for a Great Sabbat when they danced for twelve days to drive the snow away. The barrier between the worlds in thin, and spirits cross into our world, or we may slip into theirs. Solitary hawthorns growing on hills or near wells were considered to be markers to the world of the fairies. Any human who slept beneath one, especially on May Eve, was in danger of being taken away to the land of the sidhe.

On Beltane eve the Celts would build two large fires from the nine sacred woods. People would jump over them for good luck, while cattle were driven between them to purify them and increase their fertility. The ashes of the Beltane fires were smudged on faces and scattered in the fields. As at Samhain, all the household fires would be extinguished and re-lit from the need-fire. Cattle would then be taken up to the summer pastures until Samhain.

The blossoming of the apple trees marks the return of the Summer Goddess, but perhaps the most significant herald of the season is the flowering of the hawthorn. It is said that the scent of the hawthorn is reminiscent of female sexuality, perhaps the sexual flowering of the Goddess, readying herself to receive the God. In medieval England the first of May was celebrated by going out into the greenwood 'a-maying' to collect greenery and hawthorn blossoms. Love chases were customary, and the fertility of the land would be ensured by sympathetic magic; any children of these 'greenwood marriages' would be named the son of the God, hence the surnames Robin-son, Hod-son etc.

In many areas a May Queen is crowned with flowers, and her male counterpart is Jack-in-the-Green, or the Green Man. She is covered in flowers; he is covered in ivy, holly, birch, poplar, fir greenery. Once they would have been appointed by the village as representations of the Goddess and the God and their coupling ensured fertility; in some places the king and queen are still called 'the bride and groom'.

The may pole is a phallic symbol with obvious connotations of fertility and revelry. Throughout Europe there are long traditions of a stripped tree of birch erected in the village square or sacred site, decorated with ribbons and greenery. The dance around the maypole with some dancers circling sunwise, some widdershins suggests a dance of death and rebirth. It is also the cosmic axis, connecting the three realms. The hobby horse may also be the sacred steed which carries him there.

On May 1st the Padstow 'Obby 'Oss makes its annual appearance. The evening before, the village is decorated with green branches and flowers and the ceremony commences at midnight, when the townspeople sing the Night Song. The sinister black 'Oss, led by the teaser, parades through the town to the accompaniment of drum and accordion. Now and then the drum falls silent, and the 'Oss gradually falls to the floor, only to rise again. At midnight the 'Oss dies, only to be reborn at the next summer.

THEMES OF BELTANE:

- Sexuality, mating, pairing, flowering
- Jack-in-the-Green, the Green Man
- May King and Queen
- Hawthorn flowers, apple blossom
- Maypoles and phallic symbols
- Dancing, song, joy and celebration
- Hobby horses
- Closeness of the Otherworld, the sidhe, the last battle with winter
- Activity, expansion, growth
- Fire, purification

SAMPLE BELTANE RITE:
Cast the circle.

Priestess: *Lady of Summer, we call upon thee. Be with us here tonight in all your beauty and gentleness.*

Priest: *We call upon thee, Lord of the Forests, be with us here tonight in all your wildness and strength.*

Priestess: I *call upon the Lord and Lady and all here present to witness that we gather here tonight to celebrate the coming of summer, Beltane, when the Lord and Lady celebrate their sacred marriage and the earth grows fruitful from their love. We give thanks for their blessings.*

Dance and chant:
The sacred Beltane fires burn
Great wheel of life again has turned

Priest: *As the summer comes the gift of the Lord to his Lady is beauty as the earth flowers.*

Priestess: *As dead winter passes, the gift of the Lady to her Lord is summer and life.*

This is the signal for everyone to put on their summer garlands and to embrace all those present.

Bard:
O do not tell the priests of our arts, for they would call it sin,
For we will be in the woods all night
A conjuring the summer in.
And we bring you good news by word of mouth.
For women, cattle, and corn:
The sun is coming up from the south,
With oak and ash, and thorn.

Priestess: *Listen to the words of the Goddess. I am the joy of the earth and my love moves throughout all existence. Love is my law. I am all love, I am all desire. My love creates all. I am the joy in your hearts, the words in your songs. Let blessing be.*

All: *Blessed Be.*

Priest: [Points the wand at the earth as a sign of the power of the God to fertilise Mother Earth] *Life to the earth!*

There now follows a period of silent meditation.

Priestess: [Taking up the wine] I *bless this wine, the blood of the earth pressed smooth, in the name of the Lady and her Lord. I ask that as we drink of the wine, we share their love.*

Priest: [Taking up the cakes] *I bless these cakes, meal which sprang from the earth, in the name of the Lady and her Lord. I ask that as we partake of them, we share their bounty.*

Priestess: T*onight we have celebrated the coming of summer, Beltane. Only the Lord and Lady can know and measure our hearts. May they bless our hopes this night. Blessed Be.*

All: *Blessed Be.*

Cakes and wine.
Break the circle.

MIDSUMMER

Midsummer is the celebration of the summer solstice, usually around 21st June, but it (and the other solar festivals) varies from year to year, so check your almanacs.

The Saxons began their year at the midwinter solstice and the summer solstice marked its mid-point. They called the month of June *Aerra Litha* meaning 'before Litha', and July *Aeftera Litha* meaning 'after Litha'[1] leading some to speculate that the Saxon name for the festival was Litha, which is usually translated as 'light' or perhaps 'moon'. J.R.R.Tolkien used the term for a midsummer festival in the fantasy novel The Lord of the Rings and American Pagans adopted this, though it was rarely heard in the UK until the recent influx of books from the US.

This is the season when the sun is at its peak but begins to decline. It was therefore natural for people to want to protect themselves, their crops and animals from the powers of decay, winter and blight that are an inevitable consequence of the decrease of the sun's warmth and vigour. Fire, the little brother of the sun, naturally gains greater power when the force of the sun is at its best. Bonfires once blazed all across Europe and North Africa at the solstice. People leaped the fires to cleanse themselves. The fire was lit at sunset on Midsummer Eve, either with needfire kindled by the friction of two pieces of oak, or with a twig of gorse, itself a plant sacred to the sun. Men and women danced around the fires and often

1 Nigel Pennick, *Runic Astrology,* The Aquarian Press, Wellingborough, 1990

jumped through them for good luck; to be blackened by the fire was considered very fortuitous indeed. A branch lit at the fire was passed over the backs of animals to preserve them from disease.

Midsummer is a time for magic and divination. Young girls would use the magic of the season to divine their future husbands.

At midsummer foliage and flowering is at its fullest just before fruiting begins. This makes it the ideal time to gather herbs and flowers. Herbs are part of the bounty of the sun god who is always a patron of healing and medicine. Every self-respecting Pagan takes the opportunity afforded by the magic of midsummer to collect a good supply of herbs to preserve for use throughout the year. At the end of this time any herbs left over should be thrown onto the midsummer bonfire. Several plants were thought to have particular magical properties on this night, especially vervain and St. John's wort.

In Britain it was the custom to visit holy wells just before sunrise on Midsummer's Day. The well should be approached from the east and walked round sunwise three times. Offerings, such as pins or coins were thrown into the well and its water drunk from a special vessel.[ba] Wells and springs issue from the earth womb of the life-giving Goddess. Water becomes very important at the height of the summer when the growing crops need irrigating. This is also the season of necessary rain and the time of thunderstorms. While rain is always life-giving, the thunderstorms that occur in the sultry midsummer heat demonstrate the presence of the virile sky god, roaring like a bull and flashing his lightening axe. It is his semen- the rain- that fertilises the earth goddess. In some myth systems it is the thunder god who is her mate, not the sun.

Thunder gods are invariably associated with the oak tree because the oak attracts more lightening than any other tree. Thus the power of the god is mediated from the sky, through the earth realm (the tree) into the underworld via its roots. In the Craft the solar year is often seen as being ruled over by two opposing kings. The Oak King rules the waxing year while the Holly King rules the waning year. At each solstice they battle for the hand of the Goddess.

Another form of this sacred consummation takes place at the summer solstice: one perhaps more ancient still. This is the marriage of the sun and earth, of sky father and earth mother that makes the earth fruitful.

Now is the time of brightness, long days and warmth. There is the promise of the harvest growing in fields and gardens. The earth is pregnant with goodness, made fertile by the light of the sun. The Sun God is in his glory, strong, virile, the husband and lover of the Goddess. The power of the sun on this day is protective, healing, empowering, revitalizing, and inspiring. It imbues a powerful magical charge into spells, crystals, and herbs. It is a time for fun and joy, for enjoying the light and warmth.

THEMES OF MIDSUMMER

- Outdoor celebrations with group/family/friends
- Circle dancing
- Merrymaking
- Feasting
- Fires
- Torchlight processions
- Witnessing the rising and zenith of the of sun
- Bathing in healing waters
- Ritual enactment of the fertilization of the flower bride
- Ritual enactment of the marriage of heaven and earth
- Acknowledgment of the seasonal triumph of vegetation
- The battle of light and dark-Oak King and Holly King
- It is the traditional time for handfastings
- Love magic
- Divination
- Herb magic
- Sun wheels, sun, fire, bonfires, roses, rosettes, daisies, all rayed flowers, herbs, equal-armed crosses, torches.

SAMPLE MIDSUMMER RITE:

Cast the circle.

Priest:
We stand in awe beneath the Sky Father
We stand in love upon the Earth Mother
Gathered here to celebrate the rite of Midsummer,
The rite of the solstice, the rite of light on the water,
The rite of the marriage of the Sun and the Earth
The rite of awen, inspiration of bards and artists.

Bard: *This is the longest day, the time of greatest light. The powers of winter are far away, the powers of darkness a story for children. We gather to celebrate in this time of greatest light. We honour the Lord of the Sun and the Lady of the Earth whose marriage causes the grain to grow, the vine to ripen, the herbs to become imbued with power. Without their gifts we would not be.'*

Priestess: Í *call upon the presence of the Great Lady, the Earth Goddess, the Mother of the Land. We gather here in her name to celebrate this festival of growth and fruitfulness.* The woman representing the Earth Goddess steps forward.

Priest: '*I call upon the presence of the Sun God, the great archer whose arrows are shafts of light, the bright one, the all-seeing eye, the Lord of Light.* The man representing the Sun God steps forward. The priest takes the strongest hand of each and places them together, so that they stand hand in hand. The priest loops a red ribbon around their hands, but loosely and with no knots.

Priest: *On this day of greatest light when the pregnant earth blossoms with flowers and fruitfulness, we witness what the marriage of heaven and earth may achieve. Let us give honour to the joining of the sun god and the earth goddess. We honour and bless them!*

All: *We honour and bless them!*

The bard offers her a basket of green grain, unripe fruit and a loaf of bread. She holds out her hands in blessing over it and says:

Earth Goddess: *I bless the growing crops, the golden hair of the grain waiving in the wind, the burgeoning fruit on the trees and vines, the roots in the earth, the stems and buds. I bless the life in young animals and children. All this I bless in the name of the Goddess of the earth, the mother of us all.*

Sun God: *I bless the growing crops, the golden hair of the grain waiving in the wind, the burgeoning fruit on the trees and vines, the roots in the earth, the stems and buds. I bless the life in young animals and children. All this I bless in the name of the Sun God, the father of us all.*

Earth Goddess: (addressing the gathered celebrants)*Remember all of you, that you are stewards of my earth. When you abuse and defile it, you abuse and defile me. When you ravage the earth for its wealth, you rape and impoverish me. When you contaminate the earth you poison me. Be my good stewards and ever honour and protect the land as you would do honour to me. Dishonour me and you will feel my wrath in full measure. Be my good stewards and I shall reward you beyond imagining.*

Sun God: (addressing all the celebrants)*Remember all of you assembled here. You are the stewards of my gift of light and life. Always strive to bring light, healing, joy and love into your own life and into the lives of others. Remember that you are my stewards, the protectors of animals and all that is wild and free. Harm the least of these and you harm me. Dishonour me and you will feel my wrath in full measure. Be my good stewards and I shall reward you beyond imagining.*

The priest steps forward and lights the prepared bonfire (or torch if bonfires are not suitable for the spot).

Priest: *Let the fire be lit, not only here on this Midsummer Day, but also in our hearts and minds for all our lives!*

All: *May the fire be lit!*

There is now a quiet time of meditation, while all wait for inspiration to descend, or for prophecies and messages from the gods. When all are ready the fire is refreshed and fire jumping takes place as an act of purification and renewal. Food is shared and the bard begins the sharing of poetry, song and verse with a poem relating to the season. Others may add what they have learned during the time of meditation, sing a suitable song, recite a suitable verse, or read a suitable passage relating to the season and its inspirations. When all is finished the priestess pours a libation of wine to the Earth Mother (i.e. she pours some wine on the earth) and says:

Priestess: *We give thanks to the Great Mother of the earth. Mother, grant us your blessings. Grant us full orchards and fields of ripening grain. Be with us in our lives, as you once were to those of old. Grant us your love and blessings. Let blessing be!*

All: *Let blessing be!*

Priest: (holding his arms to the heavens) *Oh Lord of the Sun, great eye of the heavens! Grant you light and your blessing to this land, protect us from the powers of blight and darkness. Be with us in our lives as you once were to those of old. Grant us your wisdom and your blessings. Let blessing be!*

All: *Let blessing be!'*

Priest: *Together, brothers and sisters, we have met together to celebrate the rite of midsummer. We have witnessed the marriage of the Sun God and the Earth Mother. We have heard their blessings and done them honour. The rite is ended, let us go in peace until we meet again.*

All: *Go in peace!* The circle is broken.

LUGHNASA

The average person outside of the Pagan community has probably never heard of the festival- even in Ireland where its name survives in modern Gaelic as Lúnasa, the month of August. The ancient festival seems to have included tribal assemblies and activities extending over two to four weeks.

Lughnasa is a harvest festival, marking the end of the period of summer growth and the beginning of the autumn harvest. It is also called Lammas, from the Anglo-Saxon *hlaef-mass* meaning 'loaf-mass'. The Anglo-Saxon Chronicle of 921 CE mentions it as 'the feast of first fruits'. This first bread from the harvest was offered up as part of the Eucharist ritual.

Assemblies on hilltops are a traditional part of the proceedings. In Ireland and the Isle of Man many of these hilltop gatherings have survived to the present day. Some have become associated with Christian saints. A pilgrimage, often barefoot, would often be followed by drinking, dancing, fighting, and very unruly behaviour.

Lughnasa was a day for visiting wells. In many English villages, wells are dressed with elaborate floral tributes on various dates, but notably on the Feast of the Assumption, or Marymass, on the 15th August, four days after Old Lammas Eve. Many sacred Pagan wells were renamed after Mary, this festival and its customs are very clearly yet another example of the Christianization of earlier traditions and beliefs. In northern Scotland, where the harvest was later, Marymass replaced Lammas as the festival of the first harvest. Mary took on the characteristics of harvest goddesses depicted in robes decorated with ears of corn.

Late July and month of August are traditionally times for fairs; the weather would usually be mild and the ground suitable for travelling. Many traditional Lammas/Lughnasa fairs are still celebrated today. Many traditional summer fairs are called 'wake fairs'. A wake is a vigil kept in the presence of the body of a dead person in the period between the death and the burial. Traditionally games, feasting and drinking play a large part in the proceedings. It was also the custom to hold a wake, with a vigil and prayers, on the eve of the feast day of the local saint and follow it with a fair on the next day. Over a period of time this custom died out and all that usually remained was a purely secular occasion with much feasting and merrymaking. It seems likely that the original deity honoured with a summer wake would have been the corn god who dies with the cutting of the corn.

Lugh is said to have founded annual games to commemorate Tailtu, his foster mother, and sports are a common feature of Lughnasa survivals. The various Highland games are probably a descendant of the Lughnasa games. Some are still held around the traditional time of Lughnasa, but nowadays they may be held at any time during the summer or autumn, allowing champion sportsmen to compete at several different venues.

Even today the Irish still associate equine activities with this time of the year. It can surely be no coincidence that such famous and long-established events as the Dublin Horse Show, the Connemara Pony Show, and the Galway Races take place in late July and early August. Horse swimming is recorded as having taken place throughout Ireland. Horses were made to swim through lakes and streams at Lughnasa or on the nearest Sunday. It was thought that no animal would survive the year unless they were so drenched. A horse, as evidenced by the ceremony used to invest an Irish king, often represented the Sovereign Goddess. The Goddess was sometimes visualized as the land itself and called the Sovereign Goddess because everything that happened upon it had to have her approval or it was doomed to failure. In many cultures the earthly king was deemed to rule only through with her authority. His investiture included a symbolic marriage to the Sovereign Goddess or a real marriage to the queen who represented her. Macha, one of the triad that constitutes the Morrigan, was the horse and sovereign goddess of the Ulaidh. Her cult site was the sacred mound of Eamhain Macha (near Armagh) where assemblies were held, perhaps since the Neolithic era. *Macha* means 'enclosure' and *Eamhain* 'tumulus'. Her festival is Lughnasa, August 1st, and assemblies were held at her 'enclosure'. She was described as having golden hair, and this is clearly a reference to the corn harvested at her festival. Horses skulls were often buried beneath the threshing floor to appease the horse goddess of the land who brought forth the corn.

In parts of Ireland the nearest Sunday to Lughnasa was known as Cally Sunday. It was the traditional day to lift the first new potatoes. [1] The family would give thanks that the 'Hungry Month' of July was over, as the harvest had begun. It seems likely that the custom of first fruits would once have applied to grain.

The heliacal rising of the Dog Star, Sirius, on 27th July, marked the beginning of the Dog Days, when the sun burns at its most fierce. [2] The Dog Star follows Orion the Hunter about the sky. The ancient Greeks and Romans thought that it was a distant sun that at this time of year rose with our sun to add its own heat, making the weather unbearable. Its influence was considered baneful and malign. Hesiod described it as 'a desiccating sun', burning up plants, making the seeds in the earth sterile by depriving them of food. In Rome this month was the Heracleia, held to honour the hero-god Hercules, sometimes compared to Lugh. Like Lughnasa this festival was celebrated with games and contests.

While some writers state, without hesitation, that Lugh was a sun god [bb] others, with equal force, argue that he was neither a god of the sun nor harvest. [bc] Lugh's adventures are related in the Irish Mythological Cycle, written down by monks in the eighth and ninth centuries when elements from biblical sources and Greek and Roman myth frequently crept in. The continental Celts knew him as Lugus and his cult rose to prominence and became widespread throughout the Celtic world from the middle of the Iron Age onwards. Many place-names throughout the central and western parts of Europe provide evidence of his importance to the Celts. Lyons in France was once the capital of Gaul and was called Lugdunum, 'the

---

1 Older varieties matured later than modern ones when new potatoes are lifted in June.

2 According to Marcel Detienne (*Gardens of Adonis* p 100) The Athenian astronomer Meton dated the heliacal rising of Sirius to July 20th, but his contemporaries dated it to July 23rd or 27th, depending on whether the real or apparent rise was referred to.

Fort of Lugus', while Carlisle in Britain was Caer Lugubalion. It is possible that London, the capital city of England, was named after Lud, meaning 'the Fortress of Lud'.[3] In the Celtic world a fort may indeed be a fortified place, but can also refer to an earthwork, mound or hill associated with otherworldly characters. There is a Ludgate Hill near Saint Paul's Cathedral in London where, according to one tale, the god is buried. [bd]

The cult of Lugh was a latecomer into Ireland, introduced around the time of Christ by Gaulish or British refugees fleeing from the advancing Roman armies; there was a great migration of British Celts into Ireland at that time. [4] Lugh and his festival soon supplanted the earlier harvest lore, becoming one of the four focal points of the year in the early Irish calendar.

Lugh has several titles, including *Lámhfhada* ('long-armed') referring to his magical spear, which flashed or roared aloud when it was used in battles. The Welsh Llew is called 'the one with the skilful hand'.

Another popular misconception is that Lughnasa was a fire festival. It was not. It was associated with water and earth. Fire played no part unless you count incidental fires to cook the feast.

Lughnasa celebrates the fruition of the year's work with the weaning of calves and lambs, the ripening of the corn and the first apples, pears, bilberries, blackberries and grapes. In Ireland Lughnasa is sometimes called Bilberry Sunday. An old custom was to pick the first apples and make them into a drink called Lammas Wool.

At this point in the Wheel of the Year the Goddess becomes the Mother, who gives birth to the fruits of the land. She is Mother Nature, from whom all life emerges, who sustains all life. She is the Earth itself which bears fruit.

In the traditional Craft Lughnasa is celebrated as the festival of the God, before his decline and death with the reaping of the final sheaf of corn. It is the festival of man and 'male' energies explored through competitions, battles, warrior magic and hunting magic. It is the counterpoint to Imbolc, the festival of the Goddess, womankind, and 'female' energies explored through spinning and weaving magic, crafts and skills, poetry and bardic inspiration.

---

3 Ronald Hutton (*Stations of the Sun*) argues that it is possible that the word *lud* had another significance to the Celts, and that these cities were not named after the god at all. He contends that the worship of the god was probably not so widespread and it was a variety of local gods that were associated with Mercury.

4 Dáithí Ó HÓgáin, *The Sacred Isle,* The Collins Press, Cork, 1999. According to Dr. Ó HÓgáin at the same time the god Nuada (or more correctly Nuadhu) was also introduced from Britain, where he was known as Nodens, his principle shrine being at Lydney on the River Severn in Gloucestershire, where he is depicted as a sea god in the guise of the Roman Neptune, complete with trident. Nodens took over the role of Elcmhar as husband of Boinn and became the father of her son Aonghus who was titled *in Macán Óc* ('the young son'), paralleling the British Maponus.

In an age when crops can be imported all year round we tend to forget just how important this time was to our ancestors- the failure of the harvest meant starvation and death. This is just as true today in many parts of the world, as disturbing pictures of hungry children show us. It would be as well to remember these as we thank the gods for their bounty, and offer a prayer for the less fortunate or dedicate the celebration to them.

THEMES OF LUGHNASA

- First fruits
- The Corn God
- Bread, the first loaf of the harvest
- New wine
- The end of summer growth
- Harvesting
- Hills and harvest mounds
- Pilgrimages
- The Goddess of the Land- the Goddess of Sovereignty
- Kingship
- The Harvest Goddess
- Battles and games
- Warrior magic
- Hunting deities
- Holy wells
- Horses and riding poles

SAMPLE RITE FOR LUGHNASA

In certain branches of the traditional Craft, Lammas is celebrated as a festival of the God who, while at the height of his powers, must meet his death with the cutting of the corn. As a counterpoint to the Imbolc festival - celebrated by the women of the coven as a festival of the Goddess - Lammas is celebrated by the men as a festival of the God. However, they may decide to admit the women by consensus. If the women are permitted then they must take part as warriors in the rough games that form part of the rite. The culmination of these games is the selection of the champion who acts as sacred king in a marriage with the goddess of the land. He is marked with a tattoo that will last until Harvest Home at Hefest (autumn equinox). He promises to sacrifice himself then for the good of the land. The sacrifice he makes is that of John Barleycorn when he breaks the bread at the harvest feast, but the duty and honour of the role is very real- should he fail to keep his promise the coven and the land will suffer. The men proceed to the ritual site and set up the circle without the women. They may choose to dress as warriors with ritual woad or henna tattoos and animal totem masks or shields. The priest opens the circle wearing a stag mask.

Priest: *Lord of the Sun, the Hunt and Fire, be with us now before the time of thy departure. We call upon thee this night for this is the time of thy festival. Come unto us we beg, and honour our circle. Come, before the time of departure is upon us, come and bless this rite.*

The men now perform any magic they wish to share between themselves. This may include secrets of hunting magic, stories of the god, dances, totem work, drumming etc. The priest then steps forward.

Priest: *This is the festival of man, the hunt and the harvest which provide for the time of darkness. Yet the God stands alone without his proper consort. She must grieve for his departure and take him into the dark places. The women folk have been excluded on this night. How say you, servants of the Lord, shall we let them enter?*

If the men decide to admit the women of the coven each woman is challenged at the edge of the circle and asked what skills she brings to the assembly. She must reply according to her real skills, such as 'I am a poet', or 'I am an artist', or 'I keep the hearth fire', or perhaps if she is a policewoman, a soldier or martial artist 'I am a warrior'. If the men decide not to admit the women (though in practice it is virtually unknown for them to refuse them) they must continue the work of the night and close the circle alone. The Warrior's Cup is passed round and the games are then celebrated with contests of skill and strength. All the games are accompanied by drumming, merriment and calls of encouragement. When a champion has emerged the atmosphere becomes solemn. The champion is crowned with a wreath and swears:

Champion: *My triumph I dedicate to the Goddess of the Land. With my strength and courage I will defend the land and all upon it. With my skill and knowledge I will protect and guide my fellows. All this I swear in the name of the Goddess. This too I swear- that when the forces of dark and light stand in balance I will return and make sacrifice.*

Priest: *Witness now that our God is dying, but know that even in his death he gives his strength to the grain and his life to the harvest.*

The priest takes up the loaf and breaks it saying:
The year did spin and spring come round
While our dear Lord lay in the ground
Till rain fell thick upon his bed

And slowly then he raised his head
And grew apace till Midsummer's Day
When with his flowering bride he lay
But the year spins round and he must die
And as a seed must once more lie
We hunt him down with sharpened sickle
To pierce his heart and see blood trickle
To flay his skin from off his bones
And grind him up between two stones
Our dying Lord has lost his head
But with his death we have our bread.

He takes four fragments of bread and places one in the north, one in the east and one in the south saying at each: *Lord, give us your protection.* Each person present then eats part of the loaf. A cup of wine is blessed and passed around the circle. The circle is closed, but feasting and storytelling follow.

HERFEST

Herfest is the autumn equinox, when light and darkness stand in balance once more, with equal hours of night and day; but the darkness is gaining, day by day, and we are moving towards winter.

Herfest is a dual festival of light and darkness, joy and sorrow. It is a time of abundance when the bounty of the earth must be gathered in and safely stored against the bleak times ahead. It marks the completion of the harvest which began as early as mid-June with the hay cutting. We give the Lord and Lady sincere thanks for their gifts, but recognise that this is the time when the Lord dies and begins his journey through the underworld.

From the earliest times the farmer recognised that he worked within the powerful cycle of the seasons, and the pattern of the year which must be observed. There was a time to plant, a time to weed the growing crops, and finally, a time to harvest and collect new seeds, before the whole cycle began again. Our ancestors sought the help of the gods to ensure favourable weather- enough water to nourish, enough sun to ripen, holding back the winter frosts until the harvest had been gathered. Rituals and observances were performed to ensure such help.

The earth is the body of the Mother Goddess, venerated as the giver of life. If any drink were taken into the fields a small amount would be poured as a libation to the her - a very different attitude to today's, when pesticides and chemical fertilisers destroy the natural balance to squeeze more crops from ground impoverished by lack of proper management. An old proverb stated that a farmer should live as though he were going to die tomorrow, but farm as though he were going to live forever.

The ancestors marked this time of year with festivals dedicated to the Earth Goddess. In Greece she was called Demeter, whose name means 'Earth Mother', a goddess far older than the Olympic pantheon in which she is made the daughter of Kronos and Rhea, and sister of Zeus. She is said to have invented agriculture and the arts of sowing and ploughing, so that the fertile earth could be coaxed into bearing abundant harvests enabling humankind to leave behind a hunter-gatherer existence for a settled farming lifestyle, with the development of cities, crafts and laws.

Demeter and her daughter Persephone were often referred to as the 'Two Goddesses' or as the Demeteres. The best known story of Demeter concerns her search for her daughter Persephone ("She Who Brings Destruction") who had been abducted by Hades, the god of the Underworld. Demeter retired into her temple to grieve, and no crops grew and the earth withered. Eventually Zeus sent Hermes into the Underworld to fetch Persephone, but because she had eaten six seeds of a pomegranate while she was there, she is forced to spend six months of every year there. When she returns, the earth blossoms and spring comes. When she goes back into the underworld, we have winter. The burial of the corn dolly which is found sprouting in spring may represent Persephone.

In many parts of Greece the rites of Demeter and Persephone remained orgiastic, but in Eleusis they were celebrated as a spiritual mystery. It is possible that the grain or corn was used as an example of the mystery of death and rebirth, since Demeter gives the living the sustenance they need to survive, and the dead belong to her; the Athenians called the dead *Demetreioi*, "Demeter's people". Every fifth year, at the autumn equinox, the greater Eleusinian mysteries were celebrated, then October 4th marked the departure of Persephone to the underworld. In September candidates were initiated. According to Cicero:

> *"Nothing is higher than these mysteries. They have sweetened our characters and softened our customs; they have made us pass from the condition of savages to true humanity. They have not only shown us the way to live joyfully, but they have also taught us how to die with good hope."*

The harvest was fraught with tension; bad weather might ruin the standing crops and the work was long and hard. As late as the beginning of the twentieth century, the harvesters followed customs that would have been familiar to the ancient world. The corn was cut in decreasing circles, the Corn Spirit ever retreating into the remaining ears. There was a reluctance to be the one to cut the final ear and be the captor of the spirit, so sickles were thrown at it from a safe distance. The final severance was called 'Crying the Neck' or 'Crying the Mare'.

These last stalks were woven into a corn dolly or kern maiden, sometimes called the Ivy Girl, which contained the life-essence of the grain and which had to be kept safe throughout the winter so that life might be returned to the earth in the spring on Plough Monday. It was often tied with red thread as a form of protective magic. Sometimes the corn dolly was given a chair of honour at the harvest feast.

Into the 20th century the seasonal harvesters would elect a Harvest Lord empowered to negotiate with the farmer over terms and conditions on behalf of his fellows. As a symbol of his office, he would wear red poppies and bindweed around his hat. He would be served first at mealtimes and addressed as 'My Lord'.

Farms competed with each other to see who would finish first. The last load was taken home with great rejoicing and was followed by the harvest supper for all the workers with an abundance of good food and drink and was probably the best meal the labourers would enjoy all year. The doors and gates of the farm were decorated with greenery, corn, flowers and ribbons and wreathed scythes and sickles would be placed in the arches of the house.

At Herfest, the expansive, active part of the year is over and it is time to turn inwards. Each festival of the year in its eternal spiral can be viewed as an initiation into a new mode of consciousness. At Herfest we experience the mystery of the death of the God. Through that death comes transformation, regeneration and rebirth. It is only through this process that spiritual illumination comes. The God enters the Underworld, where he will rule as the Lord of the Dead until his rebirth at Yule. For us, it is the time for Otherworld travel and the exploration of the self. In the Underworld we encounter those aspects of the little self that stand in the way of the Initiation process. The sun's power is waning, but deprived of the external light, we encounter inner illumination.

THEMES OF HERFEST

- Harvest, abundance, bread, wine, corn, feasting
- Sacrifice of the God so that we may eat
- The mystery of death and transformation
- The mystery of the seed in the earth
- The Earth Mother and the Corn God
- Balance of light and dark
- Entering the dark half of the year
- Giving thanks to the Gods for their gifts
- What gifts have you received this year?
- What do you need to sacrifice to progress?
- What have you harvested this year?

SAMPLE HERFEST RITUAL

Cast the circle in the usual manner. The God and Goddess are invoked.

Priestess: *Harken to the purpose of this ritual and witness it, for we come here to celebrate the autumn equinox, when day and night stand in equal balance once more, and the dark is gaining. We come to give thanks for the harvest, but we come to mourn the passing of our God who dies with the cutting of the corn. But though he goes into the darkness, we remember that he shall come again.*

Bard:
The summer ebbs and lengthening shadows cloak the land
Cooling the rich earth and the ripened seeds
As day and night stand equal
And the year falls into darkness,
As the wheel turns.

We honour thee, golden-haired Goddess, Queen of the Harvest,
With your withered leaf-crown of amber, ruby and bronze;
In your right hand the sickle and in your left the glorious fruits.
The heights of the mountain and the depths of the sea ring with your voice
As you speak of death and watch the dying fire of the sun.
As the wheel turns.

We honour thee, O fallen God of the Corn, King of the Harvest
Face stained red with the failing light - marking you for sacrifice.
Black crows circle you, thrice calling your doom.
The north wind sings a lament as the Goddess raises high her sickle
And sends you to the land of the west which greets you as its Lord
As the wheel turns.

This is the final mystery we must know:
For every beginning there is an end, for every end, a beginning;
The tomb is but the earth-womb of the Mother
And the Lord of Death will return to us as the Son of Light
As the wheel turns.

Each person speaks about what the harvest means to them, what they have learned and gained this year.

Priest: *The seeds of yesterday become the harvest of today. The seeds of today become the harvest of tomorrow.*

Priestess: *God and Goddess, accept our thanks for the gifts you have given us this year. Keep us through the winter, in the dark times of our lives.*

Priest: *The God leaves us to travel through the realm of darkness. We call upon the Goddess to shelter him in her womb, and when the wheel turns, to grant him the kiss of rebirth so that he may return to his people with light and life and hope. Let the beacon be lit to celebrate out faith in his return.*

Priestess: (lighting the beacon) *The Goddess hears our prayer. The Goddess answers and the God will return.*

The group is shown 'the mystery,' an ear of corn, and asked to reflect on the cycles of life, death and rebirth. The bread and wine is blessed and shared. The circle is broken.

SAMHAIN

Samhain is the neo-Pagan festival that marks the start of winter, around the beginning of November. In the modern world, it is known as Halloween. Several ancient cultures, such as the Celts, recognised a two-fold division of the year-summer and winter. When the sun is stronger in summer and the days are longer, we have light, warmth and plentiful food as animals produce young, and plants grow. In the winter, the power of the sun declines and we have darkness and cold, vegetation dies back. Nature is in decline; hunger and death may come to many.

The festival of Samhain is known in Irish as *Lá Samhna,* in Manx as *Sauin* and *Samhuinn* in Scots Gaelic. The Brythonic languages call it the "first of Winter", in Welsh *Nos Galen-Gaeaf* in Breton *Kala-Goañv* and in Cornish *Kalann Gwav.* [be] Samhain is taken from the Old Irish for the festival samfuin from *sam* 'summer' and *fuin* 'sunset/ end'. Samhain is still the name for the month of November in modern Irish and Scots Gaelic. The earliest record we have of the name 'Samhain' comes from the Coligny Calendar, dated to the 1st century CE, a Celtic lunar calendar. Its year consists of twelve months which are divided into two groups, one headed by the month labelled *Samon* (*Samonios*) and the other by the month *Giamon* (*Giamonios*) - summer and winter. The two festivals were polar opposites; Samhain was the beginning of the winter as Beltane was the beginning of the summer. While Beltane marked the season of growth and life, Samhain marked the season of decline and death. The Celts seem to have believed that that there were two suns, the summer and the winter- one strong and hot, the other weak and cool;

perhaps even that the appearance of the summer sun in the ordinary world meant the appearance of the winter sun in the underworld and vice versa.

Modern Pagans generally celebrate Samhain on 31st October or 1st November. Others calculate the sun's cross-quarter day, when the sun has reached 15 degrees Scorpio. Others argue that Samhain should be celebrated on the nearest dark moon. However, the real astronomical marker for Samhain is the position of the Pleiades. During November the stars of the Pleiades rise in the east as the sun sets, reach their highest place in the sky - almost directly overhead - at midnight, and then set at sunrise. They can be seen in the sky for nearly the entire night. At Samhain the sun and the Pleiades are in opposition (on opposite sides of us), which happens only once in each Wheel of the Year. The Pleiades pass though the zenith of the heavens quite often, but only through the zenith at midnight on one day each year. Conversely, starting about the middle of May (Beltane Old Style) the sun is aligned between the Earth and the stars of the Pleiades i.e., the Sun is conjunct to the Pleiades, and because of this the cluster is not visible at any time of the night; and it seems to disappear from the sky for a time.

Noting and honouring the position of the Pleiades in the night sky was extremely important for the ancients, and continued to be so in many parts of the world well into the twentieth century. The ancient Greek astronomers Eudoxus of Knidos (c. 403-350 BC) and Aratos of Phainomena (c. 270 BC) referred to them as The Clusterers. Hyginus, in *Astronomica* (2.21) wrote:

> *"Our writers call these stars Vergiliae, because they rise after spring. They have still greater honour than the others, too, because their rising is a sign of summer, their setting of winter - a thing is not true of the other constellations."*

Many ancient monuments, including some British stone circles, Polynesian temples and the pyramids in Egypt and South America, were aligned to the rising of the Pleiades at October's end. In ancient Greece several temples were lined up with the rising and setting of the Pleiades, including the Parthenon and Hecatompedon for the rising, and the temple of Bacchus in Athens, and the Ascelpieion at Epidaurus and Sunium for their setting. In Mexico the Pyramid of the Sun in Teotihuacan was orientated to the setting of the Pleiades on the horizon, as were all of the city's westerly running streets. The Pleiades are also believed to be connected to the Great Pyramid of Giza; at times in history they have been perfectly aligned with the southern entrance and their light could be seen within.

The ancients used the heavens as their visible calendar, and we often underestimate the power and importance of star cycles and star myths in the ancient world. The turning stars, the course of the sun and the waxing and waning of the moon were used to plot the passage of time, in days, months, years and greater cycles still, like the fifty-two year cycle of the Pleiades midnight zenith, called a Great Year (every fifty-two years a celebration in Mesoamerica was timed to when the Pleiades were directly overhead at midnight.).

In the Doric era of ancient Greece, the calendar was also regulated by the position of the Pleiades. It had two prime times, at the beginning of May and the beginning of November, relating to the location of the Pleiades. Between May and November it was considered safe to sail, and some think the Greek name of the stars means 'to sail'. Furthermore, Hippocrates divided the year into four seasons based on the Pleiades and their relationship to the Sun and referred to the "Pleiad-month" that begins "on the day of midnight culmination" - about November 17th (near Old Style Samhain). Samhain, the Celtic festival of the dead, fell at the midpoint between the autumnal equinox and the winter solstice, and the Celts knew exactly when that was because it took place when the Pleiades culminated at midnight.

Moreover, for some, they signalled not only the Night of the Dead, but the end of the world itself. The energy of this period was considered so powerful and potentially dangerous that it was the time when major cataclysms were reputed to have happened such as the biblical flood or the sinking of Atlantis. For the Aztecs the Pleiades were Tianquiztli: 'Marketplace' or 'Gathering Place', and they linked the date when the constellation reached its highest point at midnight with the end of the world. They believed that every fifty-two years, when their 365-day sun calendar and 260-day ritual calendar came into alignment, the possibility existed that the heavens would cease to move and demons would fall from the sky. However, if the Pleiades reached their zenith at midnight and then continued harmlessly across the sky, all would be well. The Aztec and Maya not only believed that the world would come to an end on one of these Pleiades overhead-at-midnight points, but were convinced that the world had already been destroyed and recreated four times on just such a night. The end of this fifty two year cycle was celebrated with the New Fire ceremony, which involved a human sacrifice. The last recorded New Fire ceremony occurred on November 14th 1507.

The Pleiades may also represent the Seven Hathors of Egypt, the goddesses who appear at birth and death, and who in this form, are connected with doves, as the Pleiades were in Greek legend. In many mythologies, the dove or some other bird represents the soul after death, and it seems that the Pleiades were intimately connected with the mysteries of death at Samhain, and rebirth at Beltane. It may be that they were thought to guard the gates of the afterlife, opening them at Samhain so that contact with the dead could be made, or even conveying the dead souls into the afterlife during that period. In Northern European Countries there was an All Souls Day tradition of offering prayers for the dead in the direction of the Pleiades, though this was actively suppressed by the Church.

By Samhain, the grain harvest has long been gathered in, the root crops, nuts, berries and apples have been stored against the hungry winter. Animals were brought down from their summer pastures to more sheltered winter quarters, to be fed on stored hay. Any surplus animals were culled and the meat preserved. Some of the animals would have been ritually sacrificed to propitiate the powers of winter, like the Irish Formorians, gods of blight, and to feed the spirits of the dead that came to visit the Samhain feast.

With the death of vegetation and the decline of the sun, the spirits of winter, decline and death were released from the Otherworld to stalk the land. Good spirits such as the Irish Tuatha Dé Danaan and the English Puck retire from sight until spring returns. Wicked spirits, such as the Scottish Unseelie Court become very active from now until Easter along with cailleachs and hags, the crone goddesses of winter who ruled over the season. Evil omens such as black dogs and the Bean-Nighe or Washer at the Ford also appear. Sidhe mounds open at Samhain and at Hollantide (11th November- old Samhain) the Hillmen or Hogmen, the most feared of the Manx fairies, move their abode. After Samhain all the crops left unharvested belong to the sidhe. In Ireland, Halloween is called Phooka Night and after this time he renders all the crops unfit to eat and spoils all the blackberries. Welsh gryphons blight any crops left in the field after Halloween and the Lunatishee will not allow blackthorn to be cut on November 11th (Old Samhain).

The Otherworld draws close, and it is time to remember and speak to the souls of the dead. The God dwells in the Underworld as Lord of the Dead and rides out with the Wild Hunt to collect souls.

The declining sun was encouraged with bonfires. Even into Christian times, villagers cast the bones of the slaughtered cattle upon the flames. Every other fire in the village would be extinguished and re-lit from the central blaze. At the festivals where all torches and lights were extinguished and re-lit from a central bonfire (such as Samhain or Halloween), the brand was called a 'butterfly'. The Celts saw the butterfly as symbol of renewal and rebirth. The Celts suspected that butterflies might be human souls in actuality, and wore butterfly badges as a mark of respect for their ancestral spirits. It was said that the soul of a newly dead person could sometimes be seen hovering over the corpse in the form of a butterfly, and this was a good omen for the fate of the soul.

Doors and winters were left unlocked to allow the dead to enter, and a candle placed in the window to guide them. Foods were set aside for them which were not to be touched by living beings. As late as the nineteenth century in Ireland, blood was scattered at the four corners of the house to protect the dwelling from malign fairies during the winter.

It is the beginning of the time of chaos that rules until Yule and the return of the sun. The social order is reversed, and guisers play tricks and demand food.

Cross-dressing was one of the most widespread and popular ways of expressing the dissolution of the norm. In parts of Wales groups of young men in female garb were referred to as gwrachod ('hags') as they wandered through the countryside on Calan Gaeaf, indulging in all kinds of mischief.
According to the monk Bede, there were two seasons in Anglo-Saxon England. He said that summer comprised the six months in which the days are longer than the nights and winter the others. He defined when winter began, at *Winterfylleth* ('Winter Full Moon', the Saxon name for October) but not summer, which has given rise to much speculation as to whether the year's division would have run equinox to equinox or May Day to Halloween. The Northern Traditions had a major festival around 15th October (or possibly at the full moon) called Winter's Day, marking the start of winter. Like the Celtic Samhain, this festival honoured the dead. The Anglo-Saxons called November the *Blotmonath* 'Blood Month' or 'Sacrifice Month'. On November 1, rites for Hela, the Underworld Goddess, raised the dead. The next day, Odin rode his eight-legged horse through the mortal world.

Activities outdoors come to an end. Darkness returns, the year itself returns to the otherworld womb from which it came. All growth takes place in darkness from idea in the mind to seed in the ground. Here is the cauldron of Ceridwen which transforms. All things, no matter how shrunken and devitalised, can regenerate when subjected to the processes of the underworld womb as plants survive the frosts of winter. So a new cycle begins, and a chance to return to the cauldron and the blessing of the Goddess's power of transformation.

THEMES OF SAMHAIN

- Divination
- Death, culling, ending
- Feast of the Dead
- Descent into winter.
- The tomb/mound is raised over the seed
- The dark part of the year
- The Otherworld is close,
- The time of chaos begins
- Summer's end
- The dark sidhe
- Transformation through death.
- Entry to the Otherworld
- Communion with the ancestors
- The Wild Hunt
- Samhain fires
- The God of Death

- Hag Goddess/ Cailleach
- Guising
- Closing the season of agricultural work
- What is ending in you?
- What do you have inside that it is time to let go of?

SAMPLE SAMHAIN RITUAL

Cast the Circle.

Blessings be upon thee, realm of the east and air,
The whispering voice of soul and memory.

Blessings be upon thee, realm of the south and fire
Realm of Wayland's forge, where the soul is destroyed and remade.

Blessings be upon thee, realm of the west and water
Realm of Avalon, the Isle of Apples, Land of the Dead

Blessings be upon thee, realms of the north and earth
The realm of winter, barrenness and cold

Priestess:
Mother of that lives, harvester of all that dies,
Spinner of stars, weaver of worlds,
Great Goddess, we call upon you.
This is the festival of Samhain,
When barren winter approaches,
When death stalks the land,
When many are called back to your womb
To await another birth.
Be with us tonight, Dark Mother, Death Mother,
And give us sight of these.

Each person lights a candle and calls upon the name of a departed person they wish to commune with once more. This chant is sung to call back the dead:
Harken now, ye souls who wander,
Heed our call and come to the light.

Each person then offers a soul cake to the spirits. A meditation follows, during which we may communicate with the dead.

Priestess:
Ancestors; bone of our bone, seed of our seed,
We are here because you walked before us,
We are here because of your wisdom and courage,
We honour their memory on this Samhain Eve,
Our ancestors, bone of our bone, seed of our seed,
We honour you!

All: *We honour you.*

Priest:
The circle spins, the year turns from light to dark
Our Lord is the Lord of the Underworld,
Ruler of all the Mighty Dead who have gathered here tonight.
Let each of those spirits go now upon their way, harming not this world,
Travelling along the soul road towards rebirth,
Knowing we shall meet again some other Samhain Eve.
We honour them.

All: *We honour them.*

Priestess:
Dark Mother, keeper of the Cauldron of Wisdom,
We trust in the mystery of the wheel of life,
We know that the dark tomb is but your Earth womb
And we shall know rebirth and the light of another dawn.

Priestess: (takes up the cup of wine) *Blessings be upon this wine, blood of the Goddess pressed smooth, sweet and intoxicating as is her wisdom.* (It is shared.)

Priest: (Takes up the bread) *Blessings be upon this bread, body of the God, the food that nourishes us, the mystery that sustains us.* (It is shared.)

Realm of the east and air,
The whispering voice of soul and memory
Blessings and farewell.

Realm of the south and fire
Realm of Wayland's forge, where the soul is destroyed and remade.
Blessings and farewell.

Realm of the west and water
Realm of Avalon, the Isle of Apples, Land of the Dead
Blessings and farewell.

Realms of the north and earth
The cold realm of winter, barrenness and death
The womb of rebirth.
Blessings and farewell.

Priestess: *The rite is ended, blessed be.*

All: *Blessed Be.*

Break the circle.

Chapter 8
HANDFASTING

A handfasting is a Pagan wedding, usually the union of two individuals, perhaps two members of a coven or solo practitioners who meet and fall in love. The couple declare their love and commitment to each other, and promise that they will live together for a year and a day or 'for as long as love shall last' in the words of one ritual. At the end of that time, they may renew their vows, make a more permanent commitment and a legal marriage, or go their separate ways. In an age when, for whatever reason, many relationships do not last a lifetime and divorce is commonplace, it is perhaps a sensible option.

Many Pagans think that it is very important for them to be able to declare their commitment to each other in a ritual that expresses their own beliefs, feeling that a secular ceremony is not as fulfilling and meaningful as the declaration of love before their gods and their peers. The vows are usually written by the couple themselves to express their own needs and emotions. A handfasting re-enacts the great Cosmic theme of the love of the Goddess and the God and the eternal verity of human love, recreated and renewed with every lover that exists or ever existed. The pair enter the circle as two separate people, and are transformed into a declared couple, a life changing event and an important rite of passage in life's journey.

The handfasting vows are believed, literally, to be taken before the gods, and are therefore very solemn and binding. The coven or druidic grove act as witnesses, sometimes with friends and family present (if they would like to be) with the ritual presided over by a priest or priestess, druid, clan chieftain or shaman. The couple exchange vows, promising to love and honour each other, and may give each other rings, have their hands loosely tied with coloured cords or ribbons, jump over the cauldron or broomstick, and share wine together. Afterwards there are the usual congratulations, the throwing of confetti or rice, posing for photographs and a picnic or party. The handfasting may be followed by a civil wedding.

Please note that the handfasting rite may be used by heterosexual couples or partners of the same sex. It may even be adapted to encompass group marriages. The ideas in this book are only a starting point for your ceremony. Feel free to modify and change them to your needs, to write your own rituals and vows. The day is yours, so you can shape it the way you want.

The term 'handfasting' originates in the Anglo-Saxon word *handfæstung*, which meant the shaking of hands to seal a contract. A similar word exists in German and Danish. Among other things, it was applied to the act of betrothal in both England and Scotland. This betrothal itself was called, in Anglo-Saxon, a *beweddung* because the future husband was called upon to make a down payment, or *wed*, against the bride price of his lady. (This is the origin of our term 'wedding'.) The contract was sealed with a handshake or handfæstung.

In Scotland, the civil authorities recognised marriages constituted in the old style- consent to marry followed by intercourse at some later date, though the Scottish church did not. Such marriages were legal until 1940. As a result many English couples whose parents objected to their marriages crossed to the Scottish border town of Gretna Green where they could perform their own handfastings before witnesses. In Scotland the term handfasting or handfisting meant the shaking of hands to seal a contract, this might be a contract of employment, or a betrothal.

In 1820, the famous Scottish novelist Sir Walter Scott wrote of handfasting as a trial marriage in *The Monastery*:

> *"When we are handfasted, as we term it, we are man and wife for a year and a day; that space gone by, each may choose another mate, or, at their pleasure, may call the priest to marry them for life; and this we call handfasting."*

There was a custom of jumping the broom as a declaration of marriage in both Wales and England. As a child I remember an old lady saying that a couple were "living over the brush" meaning that a couple were living together without being legally married, but had a common-law relationship obtained by jumping over a broom. In Wales this was called the *priodas coes ysgub*, or broom-stick wedding.[bg]

In Wales a broom was placed on the doorstep with its handle leaning on the door frame, and the couple had to jump over it in front of witnesses. The couple were free to part within the first year, and simply had to jump over the broom again. If a child had come, the man was obliged to support it. In Caernarvonshire the practice was overseen by the oldest man in the village and the broom was constructed of oak branches and called *ysgub dderwydd* or 'druid's besom' indicating that the custom may have been very old indeed, dating back to the time of the Druids.

You need to consider the kind of vows that you will make to your beloved. Whether you will enter into the trial marriage of handfasting, or make a more permanent commitment. The traditional handfasting promises include: *I give myself to (name) for a year and a day* or *I give myself to (name) for thirteen moons.* If you make this promise, you must see it through for one year. It is a solemn vow before the Gods. If you decide to go your separate ways after a year, you might simply part, or have a formal handparting. You might not even want to make a time commitment at all, but say: *For as long as love shall last* or *While we both shall love.* This gives you the option to part before the year is up, stay together for a year, five years, twenty years, or the rest of your lives. If you decide to part, you might have a handparting ceremony if you both wish to.

If, after a year or more, you want to make a more permanent commitment, you might perform the handfasting again, saying either something like: *While love shall last.* Or if you think you really have found your soul mate, you might make a lifetime declaration such as: *For this lifetime* or *Until we are parted by death.* Once again, remember that you are making a solemn vow before the Gods, and I would urge you to think very carefully indeed before undertaking it. Though people take vows and oaths lightly in today's society and think nothing of breaking them, this is not the way of the Pagan, whose oath is made before the Old Gods, and is unbreakable, a matter of honour. If you make a solemn vow before the Gods and break it, there will be a heavy karmic price to pay, so think carefully before making any promise. A handparting is not the same as a divorce, and does not negate your oath. An oath that you make thinking that you can take it back later is not an oath, and the Gods see into your heart, even if no one else does.

Please do not even consider the entirely modern practice of soul binding, which binds the couple's souls together throughout all future incarnations as part of the rite. I believe this latter practice to be highly dangerous and very wrong. I have known people bound in this way to handpart after their year and a day, finding that their love was merely physical attraction but, calamitously, because of their soul binding, they are doomed to go throughout life after life, meeting, mating and parting in disappointment. If you are truly twin souls, then you will meet time after time anyway, perhaps not in every incarnation, but as you are meant to for your individual developments.

Remember that this is your special day, and that you should tailor it to your needs. In particular, you should create your own vows, words that express your feelings, and which will be much more meaningful than anything I could write.

HANDFASTING RITUAL

The circle is laid out as a ring of flowers by the bridesmaids. In the north, which represents the element of earth and the physical realm, they place a dish of salt and bread. In the east, which represents the element of air and the mental realm, they place a feather and the dish of incense, lighting it. In the south, which represents the element of fire and the realm of will, place a candle. In the west, which represents the realm of water and the emotions, they place a cup of water. They wait inside the circle.

The presiding priest or priestess enters the circle followed by the bride and groom, the groomsman and other guests. The groom stands to the left of the bride, the best man slightly to one side and behind him, the bridesmaid to one side and slightly behind the bride. Non Pagan guests may prefer to watch from outside the circle, but this is up to the couple, priest/ess and the guests themselves.

Priest/ess: "*We are gathered here to witness the handfasting of (name) and (name) in the presence of the Old Gods, and their brothers and sisters of the Old Ways. Be welcome all those who come in perfect love and perfect trust. We call upon our lovely Lady of the Silver Moon and our gentle Lord of the Wildwood to be present here today to bless this act of love celebrated in their honour.*

The priest/ess takes the couple and presents them to each of the quarters as follows: *Spirits of the north, you spirits of earth. Know that (name) and (name) stand before you to seek the bond of handfasting. We ask you to witness this solemn rite.*

The priest/ess takes the couple and presents them to the east: *Spirits of the east, you spirits of air. Know that (name) and (name) stand before you to seek the bond of handfasting. We ask you to witness this solemn rite.*

The priest/ess takes the couple and presents them to the south: S*pirits of the south, you spirits of fire. Know that (name) and (name) stand before you to seek the bond of handfasting We ask you to witness this solemn rite.*

The priest/ess takes the couple and presents them to the west: *Spirits of the west, you spirits of water. Know that (name) and (name) stand before you to seek the bond of handfasting. We ask you to witness this solemn rite.*

They are then led to the altar where the rings (if used) are laid on the book of rituals. The priest/ess takes up the book and rings, and says: *The ring is the perfect circle, whole and unbroken. I bless these rings in the name of the God and Goddess that they symbolise the bond of true love between (name) and (name). So shall it be.*

All: *So shall it be.*

Priest/ess: (to the man) *(name) is it your wish that you shall become handfast to (name) before the Old Gods?*

Groom: I*t is my wish to be handfast to (name) before the Old Gods and these witnesses.*

Priest/ess: *And do you pledge on your honour, and before the Old Gods and these witnesses, that you will ever strive for her happiness, placing it above your own from this day forward, for as long as love shall last between you?*

Groom: *I do so swear on my honour before the Old Gods and these witnesses that I will ever strive for (name's) happiness, placing it above my own from this day forward, for as long as love shall last between us.*

Priest/ess: *Then place your ring on her finger.* (The groom does so)

Priest/ess: (to the woman) *(name) is it your wish that you shall become handfast to (name) before the Old Gods?*

Bride: *It is my wish to be handfast to (name) before the Old Gods and these witnesses.*

Priest/ess: *And do you pledge on your honour, and before the Old Gods and these witnesses, that you will ever strive for his happiness, placing it above your own from this day forward, for as long as love shall last between you?*

Bride: *I do so swear on my honour before the Old Gods and these witnesses that I will ever strive for (name's) happiness, placing it above my own from this day forward, for as long as love shall last between us.*

Priest/ess: *Then place your ring on his finger.* (The bride does so)

The priest/ess takes the cords and fastens the hands of the bride and groom together saying: *You are bound together by the rite of handfasting in the eyes of the Old Gods and the Old Ways. Ever love and help one another as you have promised here today. May the God and Goddess bless you. So shall it be.*

All: "*So shall it be*"

The priest/ess takes the couple and presents them to each of the quarters as follows:
Spirits of the north, you spirits of earth. Know that (name) and (name) share the bond of handfasting. Bestow on them, we beseech you, your gifts of plenty, good health and fertility so that they shall always be happy together. So shall it be.

All: *So shall it be.* The couple eat some of the bread dipped in the salt.

The priest/ess takes the couple and presents them to the east: *Spirits of the east, you spirits of air. Know that (name) and (name) share the bond of handfasting. Bestow on them, we beseech you, your gifts of knowledge, good communication and inspiration so that they shall always be able to talk to each other, and find pleasure in each other's company. So shall it be.*

All: *So shall it be.* The couple are purified with the incense and are given the feather.

The priest/ess takes the couple and presents them to the south: *Spirits of the south, you spirits of fire. Know that (name) and (name) share the bond of handfasting. Bestow on them, we beseech you, your gifts of passion, vitality and creativity, so that their desire for each other shall not wane. So shall it be.*

All: *So shall it be.* The couple light the candle, holding the taper together.

The priest/ess takes the couple and presents them to the west: *Spirits of the west, you spirits of water. Know that (name) and (name) share the bond of handfasting Bestow on them, we beseech you, your gifts of friendship, support and love. So shall it be.*

All: *So shall it be.* The couple both drink from the cup and are led back to the altar.

Priest/ess: *Let all of us now offer blessings and congratulations to (name) and (name).* Everyone speaks any prepared or spontaneous blessings they have and showers the couple with flower petals. The broom is brought forward and the couple encouraged to jump over it for luck.

Priest/ess: *As it has been since the beginning of time, and as it shall be till the end, two lovers have been joined together, and by this have been made stronger, happier and greater than they were apart, and the simple fact that their love exists in the world benefits us all. This wondrous state is the gift of our gracious Lady and her own gentle Lord, whose love flows through all things, and whose passion we see reflected throughout the seasons, and which is the deepest mystery of our faith.*

The bridesmaids open the flower circle.

Priest/ess: "*The circle is open but unbroken. What we have witnessed here today will remain in our hearts. We thank the spirits of north, south, east and west for their presence. We thank our gracious Lord and Lady for their blessings. Blessings be on all. So shall it be.*"

All: *So shall it be!* This is the signal for the feast and games to begin.

RENEWING THE VOWS

If the handfasting vow is for a year and a day, then the vows should be renewed after that time elapses. Another full ceremony can be held, with coven and witnesses present or it may be a simple exchange of vows between the two people concerned.

This time the couple may wish to make a more permanent arrangement or merely renew the arrangement for another year and a day. Otherwise, the handfasting lapses after thirteen moons and the couple is free to go their separate ways with no recriminations. If both people agree, then a handparting ritual may be held to bring closure to the relationship.

HANDPARTING

With all the best will in the world, relationships sometimes do not work out. The couple may simply go their separate ways, hopefully without recrimination or blame, or choose to undergo a formal handparting ceremony. One partner should not force the other into this, and it should only be done if both parties are on friendly enough terms to undertake it with good will, to bring closure to the relationship, and allow each to move on.

HANDPARTING RITUAL

The candles and the altar should be black, which is the colour of Saturn and the colour of endings. One lit black candle, representing the ending relationship, is placed on the altar, flanked by two unlit blue candles for healing. The couple hold the ends of the cord they were originally bound with for the duration of the ceremony, until it is cut by the celebrant. A very sharp knife or shears are placed on the altar for this purpose.

The celebrant cats the circle in the usual manner and announces: *We are here to mark the handparting of (name) and (name) who wish to separate from each other at this time.*

Celebrant addresses the wife: *(Name) have you come here of your own free will to seek handparting from (name).*

Wife: *I am.*

Celebrant then addresses the husband: *(Name) have you come here of your own free will to seek handparting from (name).*

Husband: *I am.*

Celebrant: *Then let you be parted without recrimination or blame, neither seeking ill for the other. Remember that this has been one of life's lessons, and youi have learned from your relationship. Cherish the memory of good times you have shared, and relinquish the pain. (Name), are you willing to do so?*

Wife: *I am.*

Husband: *I am.*

Celebrant: *I declare before the Lord and Lady and your brothers and sisters of the Craft, that you are no longer handfast.* S/he cuts the cord they hold between them. *Let each of you take your own blue candle, which represents the healing journey each of you must now take.* They each light their separate candle from the black central candle, which is them extinguished as a sign that the relationship is finally over. The cords and this candle are burned in the fire, either now or later, by the celebrant.

Celebrant uses the incenses to cleanse the aura of each saying: *Forget painful thoughts and remember each other kindly.*

Celebrant: makes the sign of the pentacle before each with their blue candle: *Let anger and hatred burn away.*

Celebrant: sprinkles each with water saying: *Be cleansed of heartache and regret.*

Celebrant places a few grains of salt in each of their palms: *Return to the world and take up your life anew. The rite is ended. Go in peace.*

The handparted couple then walk to opposite quarters of the circle and exit in different directions.

Chapter 9
NAMING CEREMONIES

Cast the circle or create a sacred space and invite the quarters and Lord and Lady.

Priestess: *We are gathered here today in joy to celebrate the birth of a child to … and…. In the presence of this community we welcome him/her.*

Priest: *Have you chosen a name for your child?*

Parent: *Yes, his/her name is…*

The priest leads the parents carrying the child to the four quarters in turn:

Priest: *Guardians of the east, bless this child …with intelligence and inspiration.*

Guardians of the south, bless this child … with vitality and a passion for life.

Guardians of the west, bless this child … with love.

Guardians of the north, bless this child … so that he/she may never know hunger and want.

Priestess: *May our Gracious Lady and her Gentle Lord watch over …, protect and guide him/her until the time comes for him/her to choose his/her own path.*

Priest: *The Lord and Lady have blessed you with the gift of a child. How will you honour that gift?*

Parents: *I promise that I will always love and support … to the best of my ability. I will try to create a loving, cheerful home in which to raise ... I promise that I will always ready to listen to …. and honour the choices he/she makes. I promise I will teach …honesty, generosity of spirit and tolerance. I will do my best to teach my child about responsibility so that he/she may live in this world with honour. So mote it be.*

All: *So mote it be.*

The child is taken round the circle to receive the individual blessings and gifts of its members.

Close the circle.

Chapter 10
FUNERALS/ MEMORIAL SERVICE

Priestess: *We are gathered here today to celebrate the life of … who has gone from us to the Summerlands. We come to take our leave.*

Priest: *Life is a circle. We are born from love, we flourish and grow. We love and touch the lives of others, we move in the flow of life. But the wheel turns, and each of us must embrace the final mystery. The Goddess enfolds us once more, and we sleep in her arms until another dawn.*

Priestess: *Without death, there can be no rebirth, and this is the way of the wheel. Death has not taken … from us, for he/she remains in our hearts and memories.*

Beginning with the chief mourner, people speak of the deceased, telling stories of them, playing their favourite music, and reading poems that express their feelings.

Priest: *…has left us for a time, the work of his/her life completed. Now …dwells in the Summerlands in youth, and strength and beauty. We will see him/her again. We rejoice in the knowledge that time is no barrier and that friendship endures.*

Priestess: … *we wish you perfect love and perfect happiness. You have touched out lives, and we will never forget you. Do not forget us, but greet us when we meet in the Summerlands. So mote it be.*

All: *So mote it be.*

Follow the ritual with food and drink.

Chapter 11
INITIATION
THE PATH OF THE PRIEST AND PRIESTESS

The Craft is a mystery tradition that has formal degrees of initiation. In this, it differs from most other forms of modern Paganism.

Some Pagans condemn covens for their exclusivity, their systems of degrees and their titles of high priest and high priestess. This criticism is understandable when we have characters like Lady Tiggywinkle, who read a book on the Craft a year ago and now she is a high priestess and has even written her own book about it. Or Darth Moloch who is magus of his own dark coven – or at least he is when his Dad lets him stay out late. Such people have always existed of course, and are found in every branch of Paganism, but it is true to say that the Craft, with its hierarchies and titles, is a magnet for the egomaniacs and lunatic fringe.

However, the Craft degree system - and its hierarchy - provides a stable and firm foundation to assist individual spiritual progress. Candidates are enabled to develop at their own pace by a supportive group setting, under the guidance of an experienced teacher. As they progress, they become able to train and help the less knowledgeable – with each degree comes greater responsibility. Those groups that try to run as democracies where those with no know-how have as much say as those with a great deal, or those groups run by inexperienced [and all too often inflated-ego] individuals with no proper training tend to fall apart very quickly, as do those groups where people are advanced too quickly through the degrees. Over the many years I've spent in the Craft, I've learned the hard way that the traditional coven set-up is the by far the best way of organising and running a magical group. Every time I, in my ignorance or arrogance, have deviated from its rules, the consequences have been disastrous.

Working in a group can be very powerful and members can come to see each other as family. It can fall apart with power struggles and individual personality clashes. The way to avoid this [at least as far as this is possible] is to set up the group properly. Meet an interested person and invite them straight in, and you are asking for trouble. Short of a high priest? There's a bloke who started coming a couple of weeks ago, never mind he isn't experienced or initiated, we need one don't we? Sleep with all your neophytes and it really isn't going to last. This is all juvenile behaviour unworthy of a serious magical group.

Magical groups can be large or small, but I think the optimum number lies between ten and sixteen, if possible with balanced numbers of men and women [leaving aside exclusive men's and women's rituals] for balance. Larger groups tend to break up, and this may be the natural order of things, generating new groups, though it can be a case of trying to balance too many personalities and aims. When admitting a person into a group, be aware that you are adding their energies to the pattern, to the group mind, and they must be harmonious with group aims.

Everyone has their strengths and weaknesses in the magical arts – some have easier contact with the spirit realms and make good Fetches, others can weave the energies of the group during ritual and make good Weavers. Hearth Witches bring in the energies of the plant kingdom, and the Crowman stands as guardian of the gates and protector in the spirit world. A high priest needs to take on a pastoral role as well as a ritual role, and needs to be liked and respected for his compassion, common sense and natural wisdom. A high priestess needs to be a bloody good organiser as well as a good ritualist. The more skilful each of the members is, the more effective the group will be. A balance of various abilities is necessary to make an effective magical group.

Sadly, just getting together a group of like-minded friends is one of the worst ways to found a magical group. The most effective groups are drawn from a variety of people with diverse backgrounds who probably didn't and wouldn't know each other if not for their involvement but who, after a while, become closer than family.

Setting up a Hearth and coven in the proper way takes a long time and a lot of hard work. I reckon it takes at least ten years to get an effective coven off the ground, maybe more, but the results are a million miles beyond what you can expect from a loose-knit collection of interested parties. Michael Howard once came up with a good image of how a magical group is formulated- the Tudor Rose. If you've forgotten your history lessons, this is the combined red rose of the House of Lancaster which forms the larger, outer petals and the white rose of the House of York forming the inner petals. As a representation of a magical group, the red petals are the outer court or aspirants, the inner white petals the coven, and the golden stamens at the centre are the initiates at the core of the Hearth.

The Craft is a mystery religion, and a system of initiation through various degrees is implicit, and in this it follows very ancient principles. The word 'mystery' comes from the Greek *musterion* meaning a secret rite or doctrine. A follower of the mysteries in ancient Greece was a *mystes* or 'initiate', a term originating in the word *myein* meaning 'to close' or 'to shut' i.e., to close or shut the eyes and mouth, since only initiates were allowed to observe the rituals and these were not to be spoken of to the uninitiated. In the ancient world, the mysteries were not open to everyone, but only to those who were properly trained and prepared, those who were mature and responsible enough to approach them with due reverence and ready for the profound inner changes it would create.

Initiations centered around the theme of death and rebirth, the candidate undergoing the same journey as the God or Goddess; thus the candidates became the 'twice-born'. They followed the same basic pattern that most Craft initiations follow today, first with training, then the rite proper with ritual purification, warnings and challenges, an ordeal, a binding oath, revelation of the deity and secret symbols, rebirth and consecration as an initiate, followed by a proclamation of the new status of the candidate to all assembled.

Reputable covens ensure that the training for priesthood is thorough and monitored at every stage so that the priest/ess is ready for the degree conferred, is effective, competent, and works connected to the Gods. This training is difficult and requires a high level of commitment over many years. Most people are not willing to put in the time and effort, and this is the main reason why initiation is reserved for a few.

Putting aside those traditions that 'initiate' new members as soon as they arrive [in which 'initiation' is merely an acceptance into the coven and signifies nothing more] initiation confirms that the candidate has completed adequate training and achieved sufficient spiritual advancement as will enable them to function as a priest/ess.

Many beginners think that initiation is conferred by the ceremony, and that the person involved is thus promoted to a higher rank rather like an army officer. This is far from the truth. The neophyte, having undergone training and taken part in various rituals and spiritual practices, starts to experience a heightened state of consciousness and awareness. He or she is often very confused at this stage, suddenly aware of entities, archetypes, spirits, concepts and ideas that may seem contradictory and confusing. Many people take fright at this point and back away, but providing that the candidate handles this properly, accepting guidance from the elders, initiation will occur as a fundamental change of consciousness, a progression to the next stage. An experienced high priest/ess will recognise when this juncture is reached, and the candidate will be formally initiated: a ritual and magical event that triggers the next stage in the process.

At this point the initiation may fail, leaving the candidate in a spiritual limbo. This can happen for one of two reasons. Firstly, unless the candidate is set, properly prepared and ready to receive and return the power, no initiation can take place; Plato remarked "*Many who beat the wand, but few who become Bakchoi.*" [bh] Secondly, if the initiator is not in contact with the spiritual forces, he or she will fail to initiate the candidate.[bi] There are plenty of people out there claiming higher degrees who don't even realise they have never had a true initiation.

Initiation is a death and rebirth not symbolically, but in a very real sense. In some tribal societies, the candidate is thought of as a ghost for the duration of the process, until the new birth takes place. He might be buried or coffined in some way, returning to the primordial earth-womb of the Goddess. Often, the initiate identifies himself with the reborn god. In Egypt, for example, in one initiation ceremony described in the Leyden Magical Papyrus, he 'participated' in the reconstitution of the scattered body of Osiris, and was reborn with the reincarnated god.[1] The old self can never be reclaimed, and a new self emerges from the old shell: the process is traumatic. It is said of several mountains in Wales, that if one were to spend a night there, one would either come down mad, or a poet [i.e. a bardic initiate]; true initiation is a harrowing process, and one which may lead equally to enlightenment or madness.

This threshold point was deliberately provoked in the initiation rituals of some mystery schools, when the candidates were put through terrifying ordeals involving burial or entombment for days, or being led through the darkness of a labyrinthine cave. In tribal cultures, suffering may be deliberately induced to mimic the crisis which sometimes triggers a shamanic initiation. Shamans may experience 'death' by being entombed for up to seven days, during which they experience being dismembered by demons before being re-assembled with new bodies that contain psychic powers. In all parts of the world the dawning of the shaman's enlightenment begins with a 'shamanic crisis', often in adolescence, but sometimes much later.[2] This is a severe illness or breakdown which actually threatens his life, and he lingers for a time between on the threshold of life and death. The shaman is reduced, by the trauma of this incident, to a primal way of thinking and being, and only then can he enter the archetypal primordial state where humans can converse with gods, animals and plants. He experiences the sensation of dissolution and the separation of body from spirit, something that only usually occurs in physical death, and which cannot be compared to astral travel or out of body experiences, or even an initiation in other magical traditions.

Returning from his crisis, the shaman knows, from his own encounters, that the world is alive, that everything has spirit and that we are surrounded by spirits, a viewpoint called animism by anthropologists. When he interacts with the world of spirit, he is practising shamanism, and only then. He may work with a variety of supernatural beings and from these learn how to cure specific illnesses, divination, the mastery of fire, weather magic, hunting magic, the retrieval of lost souls or the accompanying of the souls of dead to the Otherworld, and the removal of curses. He can travel great expanses in spirit flight, hear what is going on at a remote place, send messages over a distance and even shapeshift. Furthermore, he may take on the role of the priest of a community, becoming the bridge between the world of spirits and humankind.[3]

Plutarch commented that the soul at the point of death undergoes the same experience as those who have been initiated into the great mysteries:

---

1 Christian Jacq, *Magic and Mystery in Ancient Egypt*

2 In some places, the role of shaman is hereditary, but only if the spirits have chosen the successor, and he has undergone the crisis.

3 Anna Franklin, *Path of the Shaman*, Lear Books

"...at first wandering to and fro, and journeys with suspicion through the dark as one uninitiated, and then come all the terrors before the final initiation, shuddering, trembling, sweating, amazement: then one is struck with a marvellous light and is received into pure regions...and bearing his crown joins in the divine communion... and the initiate beholds the uninitiated ...huddled together in mud and fog, abiding in their miseries through fear of death and mistrust of the blessings there."

We can find many such descriptions of initiations in the ancient accounts, in stories from shamanic cultures, but also in more recent times here in Britain, deriving from the shamanic traditions of our Celtic and Anglo-Saxon ancestors (see my *Path of the Shaman* for a more full account of this).

Not every aspirant will gain true initiation in this lifetime. If a person encounters many difficulties in the path of initiation the Gods may be telling them they are not ready, or it may just be that they are being tested to see whether they are committed enough to overcome any obstacles. The Gods often interfere in someone's life to point them in the right direction, or deter them from following the wrong path for them. This is why barriers are placed in the path of the would-be initiate, sometimes by the Gods, and always by the coven. Tests are made ensure the suitability of the candidate - who might not even be aware that they are being tested. In our coven, quests are given that must be pursued and resolved before initiation is even considered.

In our Hearth we do not recognised initiation by another group, since the candidate has not been magically connected with the coven's Otherworld guides and the reservoir of knowledge of the tradition that resides in the Otherworld, nor are they plugged into the group mind of the coven. People who have been initiated by another tradition may resent being asked to undergo further training and another initiation, but we think this absolutely necessary. When I joined the Coranieid I was re-initiated after ten years in the Craft.

We do not recognise self-initiation at all. This is not to say that self-initiation is impossible, but successful self-initiation is rare. When people talk about self-initiation, they generally mean what we would refer to as Dedication, a promise to honour and love the Gods and learn of them. True initiation is something much more profound. I'm not even sure it is possible to be your own teacher – you are trying to teach yourself something you do not know, and this is a paradox. It is true that the real teaching comes from the Gods and spirits, but until you have learned how to contact them, how to recognise illusion and self-delusion from truth, this is fraught with danger. Furthermore, the changes the process effects are very difficult to deal with alone. An experienced high priest or priestess will be able to guide the initiate through the stormy waters. A person can never initiate themselves into a tradition from which they have never had training or approval.

It must be remembered that initiation is not an end goal and the candidate is not perfected at the point of initiation; it is a mark post on the journey of the spirit which is a continuing succession of trials, revelations, back-sliding and progress.

THE DEGREES

Three degrees of initiation are a common feature in many mystery traditions. When the great mysteries of Eleusis were at their height in ancient Greece there were three grades involved: the lesser mysteries open to all; the great mysteries of initiation and lastly Epoptism, of which Plutarch said that one could not hope to penetrate its mystery until late in life.

The three degree system in the Craft is popularly thought to have been introduced by Gerald Gardner from Freemasonry, but in *The Discoverie of Witchcraft*, written in 1584, Reginald Scot described three levels of initiation as being common among witches of the time. The first was a public ceremony when a person was made a witch. The second and third ceremonies took place privately with the leader of the coven. During the second ceremony the person made vows to observe the commandments of 'the devil' [the Horned God], while the third ritual described seems to have been akin to the Great Rite. After the latter two, the initiates were responsible for performing magic and recruiting others into the Craft.[bk]

I like to think of the three degrees of the Craft as being akin to mediaeval guild apprenticeships. A person wanting to learn a particular trade would have a trial period with a craftsman and then if they showed some skill and dedication, they were accepted into the guild as an entered apprentice, working under a master craftsman. When they had acquired enough knowledge and skill they would become a journeyman, someone able to go off and do a job without needing to be supervised all the time. Eventually, they would become a master craftsman, able to take on apprentices of their own.

In reality, our own system of initiation is five-fold. The first level is that of dedication which is achieved after a period of probation in the coven. The first degree marks the achievement of priesthood, an admission to the tradition. The second degree confirms the journeyman stage, where the initiate is fully capable of conducting rituals unsupervised. The third degree makes the initiate a high priest or priestess, capable of running a coven and taking on apprentices. The third degree may or may not trigger the dawning of the fourth, which is rarely taken and even less rarely achieved.

Each degree is protected by a Guardian of the Threshold. This is not a priest/ess within the rite, but the part of the self that bars the way to that initiation: something which has to be confronted and dealt with. The Guardian of the first degree is fear, the guardian of the second is ego, the third is duality, and the fourth is physical death.

What follows is an outline of how the degree system is conducted within our Tradition. Please bear in mind that traditions vary greatly, and other witches will organise their systems very differently.

THE OUTER CIRCLE

Many covens run an outer circle or outer court, a teaching meeting open to interested people wish to explore the Craft as a possible path. This is the best way of finding new members by the coven, and by far the best way of finding a coven for anyone looking. It gives covens the opportunity to get to know potential members, and an opportunity for potential members to test whether a particular tradition is right for them. Members of an outer circle or outer court are sometimes called cowans.

We hold an outer circle on a monthly basis. In it, we teach the basics of the Craft and related Pagan subjects. We ask that someone attends the outer circle for at least a year before they ask for admission to the coven. In this way, we can see just how committed someone is and whether they are likely to contribute to the coven and fit in with its energy patterns, or whether they are dilettantes, ego driven or just plain nuts. A person who seems perfectly sane and amiable over a few chats in the pub can turn out to have a lot of personal problems and destructive behaviour. Anyone who wants everything now is never going to be a good coven member or magician.

PROBATIONER

If a person is accepted into the coven, they begin as a probationer and remain so for at least a year. What they think the Craft involves and what it truly is may be very different, and they may realise it is not their path, they may not be able to find the time and make the commitment it demands, or may just be unable to cope with the cold and discomfort of winter rituals!

DEDICATION

After serving in the coven for a year, someone should have more or less decided whether the Craft is for them. They may leave, be requested to leave, or ask to become an accepted neophyte of the tradition - or dedicate - and begin training in earnest.

During the rite of dedication, the aspirant promises to respect the Tradition and its teachers, to honour the God and Goddess, to learn all they can and to keep the knowledge secret. In our coven, dedicates wear a white cord.

The Work of the Dedicate

- The dedicate should attend all the meetings they are required to [this might consists of the eight festivals, any esbats the coven holds, and perhaps outer circle training meetings and specific dedicates' training meetings] unless there is a valid reason they cannot. This tests commitment.
- They should learn the basics of the Craft – the eight festivals, the eight paths, the meaning of the elements and quarters, the Gods, the principles of ritual, the five essentials, the web, spirits of place and so on.
- The dedicate needs to work on understanding him/ herself. This is probably the most important thing of all at this stage. The old occult dictum, written above the door at Eleusis, is 'Know Thyself', since without this, no progress is possible.
- Dedicates take a greater part in ritual than a probationer and by this method learn about ritual.
- They should make their magical tools with full intent and understanding.
- They should help out probationers and outer circle members where possible.
- They should respect that which is taught and those who teach it, and 'keep silence' to non-coven members about coven business.
- The dedicate learns to gather and hold personal power
- The dedicate learns to maintain a sense of connectedness within rituals.
- He or she learns to still the mind, concentrate and focus during meditation and ritual.
- The dedicate pursues the quest they have been given.

FIRST DEGREE INITIATION

By the time we initiate someone, we have weeded out those who are simply attracted by the image and the title 'witch'. Initiation is a profound commitment to the Craft and coven and should not be undertaken lightly. While a dedicate may leave the Craft, the first degree initiate is a priest/ess for this lifetime, even if they do not practice.

Broadly speaking, first degree initiation is available to all those who have completed a successful period as a dedicate. Everyone in the coven has the opportunity to become a priest or priestess. However, the degree will not be conferred until the candidate is ready. This is assessed in the following manner by the High Priest and High Priestess:

- The candidate has shown commitment and loyalty to the coven by attending such meetings and festivals as they are required to. [The candidate may have shown even greater commitment than this by being involved in other meetings and Hearth activities, which is a good indication that they will be a committed priest or priestess.]

- The candidate has demonstrated an understanding of how rituals work, how to behave within a circle, and they have fitted into the energies of the circle
- They have gained some proficiency in channelling magical energies
- They are aware of, and interact with, the world of spirit.
- The candidate has made their tools.
- The candidate has demonstrated an understanding of the Tradition and honoured the Old Gods.
- The candidate has respected the Hearth structure and observed its principles.
- The candidate has demonstrated to the HP and HPs that they have undertaken a personal journey throughout the period as a dedicate, dealing with personal fears, problems and hang-ups.
- The candidate has demonstrated that they have progressed in spiritual matters and have begun to forge Higher Plane contacts.
- They have learned to enter into 'ritual consciousness' and the group mind.
- They have completed their dedication quest.

The Symbol

The symbol of the first degree is the downward pointing equilateral triangle. It is one of the tasks of the initiate to meditate on this emblem. The triangle is one of the strongest shapes used in building; it spreads load evenly and since all pressure is put on the angles of a triangle evenly, it balances loads [bl] just as the initiate is called upon to do.

It represents triplicities such as: the father, the mother and the child; heaven, earth and underworld and mind, body and spirit.

It is a truly ancient representation of the womb of the Goddess, femininity and female sexuality. According to Marija Gimbutas, in the ancient Mediterranean it represented the vulva, birds, water and life-giving nourishment from the moisture of the Goddess's body - her breasts, eyes, mouth, and vulva. [bm] In Tantric Hinduism it was the primordial *yoni* [vulva], existing before the universe began, and where the Goddess conceived the spark of life, the *bindu*, which was born as the male principle, symbolised by the upward-pointing triangle. In the Craft too, the downward pointing triangle symbolises the Goddess, and is sometimes called the chalice [which in itself represents her womb] and water, while the upward triangle, sometimes called the blade, represents the God and fire.

The Initiation

Initiation fundamentally changes a person. The old self dies so that a new self, a priest/ess and witch, may be born. It is a process which begins within the candidate but which culminates in the ceremony of initiation, when the candidate is put in contact with the coven's Otherworld guides, but which may continue for several months or even years. It can be very painful as the old self is stripped away and the birth pangs of the new self are felt.

This can involve not only integrating the new consciousness, but also balancing the requirements of everyday life with the demands of spiritual progress. This can be a difficult line to tread. Often family members who are not involved become resentful of the time taken by its commitments. Spouses may even suspect that their partners are getting up to no good with coven members of the opposite sex, or just upset that their partner has found a life-changing interest that doesn't involve them and are made insecure by the changes. Those with supportive partners and families are very lucky. This is a delicate balancing act for many coven members. We have had a priestess who was forced to leave the coven when her husband made it too difficult for her to stay, and another who got divorced in order to continue in the Craft.

Though Gardnerian and Alexandrian witches are required to enter this ceremony naked to reflect the vulnerability of a new-born, the Traditional Craft has always worked robed. In our tradition, to symbolise the fact of death and rebirth, the candidate is asked to prepare their own tomb, actually a barrow made of earth and branches. Though a similar method is used in modern rebirthing practice, this is an ancient technique used in initiation ceremonies.

The candidate enters his tomb, conscious of having left behind all that has gone before, 'dying' to the old life, before lying suspended between life and death for several hours. During this time they await a vision which will guide them over the coming months and years.

They are then led, blindfolded, to the circle. This is an act of trust. Their shepherd must lead them through branches, brambles and tangled roots and they must allow themselves to be led, trusting that that won't be injured and will be taken to the right place. Entering into the rite involves abandoning this control and surrendering to the process. Letting go of control is very difficult for most people, and learning to trust fellow members of the coven is very difficult in a world when betrayal and mistrust is an everyday event. Inside the circle and inside the coven, we must only act from pure motive of 'perfect love and perfect trust'. As Vivienne Crowley puts it:

> *"The coven is the image of the God and Goddess and must be made in their image. It is a home, a place of wholeness, truth and love in which we can grow to spiritual maturity".*[1]

---

1 Vivianne Crowley, *Wicca*, The Aquarian Press, Wellingborough, 1989

The candidate is then taken to a gateway opened in the western quarter of the circle, the gateway of death, the dwelling place of the Ancestors, reminding them that they stand in the realm of death, awaiting rebirth. They are told that their life journey has brought them to the point, a moment of focus to which all paths have lead, and from which all paths will follow. Most people have gone through a lot of soul searching and questioning before they even seek out a coven, before they even become a Pagan. They have tried various paths any maybe even other religions. They have looked deep within and sought answers to life's questions. If they wanted easy answers in ready-made truths dispensed by others, they would have wandered off again, since the Pagan must seek his own answers.

At the edge of the circle they are challenged and warned of what will follow if they proceed – that they will face challenges and perils in their lives henceforth. They are asked if they want to go back and refuse the initiation. They are warned that they must come forward of their own free will, no one assisting in any way. They are not lifted over the threshold, helped or carried- they must take that step for themselves with determination and courage in their hands, aware that their fate is their own choice.

If they elect to continue, the blindfold is removed so that they emerge from the darkness into the light of the circle.

They are asked what they seek within this degree, and the candidate must have reflected on what they really seek. Is it knowledge for its own sake? Is it power over others? Or is it the path of the wise?

The oath to the Craft is taken, but only after another warning that it is a difficult promise to stand by, one that brought torture and death to those in the past, and one which still brings persecution today. The candidate is given yet another opportunity to withdraw. The oath, in the name of the coven's Gods, promises to respect the tradition and the knowledge given, to hold it secret and not to use it in any evil manner. The secrecy in the Craft is criticised by those who do not understand the reasons for it. Firstly, we protect the identity of coven members unless they wish otherwise. Even today, Pagans are open to persecution by religious fundamentalists, and may face difficulties in the workplace or by family members.

When the oath is taken, the initiate is anointed as priest/ess and witch, and given the red cord which symbolises initiation, and the lineage. A new name is taken, since they are now new born, one they will use within the circle. They are taken by the waist and introduced by this name to the powers of the circle and the Gods. They then consecrate the ritual tools they will use as a practising witch.

The results of initiation are profound, and throw the new initiate off balance until the new world-view is assimilated. This disturbance may take the form of a rejection of the group or Craft for a time, and sometimes resentment is felt towards the initiator, or the high priest and high priestess. If the initiate rejects what they have been given, or is not really ready for what is passed to them, a nervous breakdown can be the result. I once made a bad mistake of this kind when I was younger, and initiated a man who proved to be emotionally unstable, when I had thought him just to be a little over-enthusiastic. He then proceeded to destroy the coven and his own wellbeing in the process.

People expect that after they have gone through an initiation they will suddenly acquire greater magical powers. This is not the case. In fact, the candidate may feel empty, resentful and confused after the ceremony. He or she will soon realise that the ritual has confirmed what is already happening, and given them the keys to the next doorway.

The Work of the First Degree

- The initiate continues to learn from the elders on the physical plane, and the spirits of Gods and ancestors on the spiritual plane.
- The work of the first degree priest or priestess is concerned with mastering ritual, learning more of the magical process and taking a much greater part in performing ritual, including casting the circle and invoking the directions. He or she may invite the God or Goddess to be present in the circle but not invoke them.
- He or she will begin to specialise in one of the Eight Paths of Magic. He/she may work as a healer of some kind, or perhaps as a bard, sacred dancer, hearth witch, warrior or shaman, etc. depending on his or her natural talents.
- It is the duty of the first degree priest to take his/her priestly work into the larger community, providing some teaching for other members of the Hearth, especially probationers and the outer circle, at the discretion of the Elders.
- He or she will attend initiates' meetings for further training. Initiates' meetings may also discuss new admissions to the coven, dedications and other matters as they arise, but any final decisions are taken by the coven leaders.
- A new quest is given which must be completed before second degree initiation can take place.
- The first degree develops a greater understanding of the tenets of the Tradition.
- He or she develops a greater kinship with and respect for nature.
- He or she must act in all things from the principle of Perfect Love and Perfect Trust.

SECOND DEGREE

Many people never advance beyond first degree, but after the completion of the first degree quest, a priest or priestess may be allowed to undergo the second degree initiation. The initiation makes them a coven elder. It should only be undertaken by those who have the necessary Will, courage, strength, ability, commitment, time and dedication to the Craft.

We have several names and allegories for this degree, including 'the Siege Perilous' named after the seat at the Round Table that could only be used by the Perfect Knight, and which destroyed any other that sat there. At a true second degree, the Gods may test the fitness of the candidate to the limits of their endurance.

The Symbol

The symbol of the second degree is the inverted pentacle - the world turned upside down, because this is often precisely what happens to the candidate. It indicates that the four physical elements [and earthly considerations such as position and ego] still dominate spirit, the fifth element.

The Initiation

This happens to some extent in all the initiations, but the second degree seems to be the most dangerous [apart from the fourth]. Any hidden weaknesses and faults will be brought to the surface and have to be dealt with. The results of true initiation are profound, and throw the new initiate off balance until the new world-view is assimilated. This disturbance may take the form of a rejection of the group or Craft for a time, and sometimes anger and resentment is felt towards the initiator or the high priest and high priestess. Such a person may have been making rapid progress, and be disillusioned by the fact that there is a great deal more to come. Progress may have been at an intellectual, rather than a spiritual level, and while it is important to work on a mental level, this is insufficient.

We also call the effects of the second degree 'the Dark Journey', since the candidate will go through a 'dark night of the soul' experience during the process, in which everything is questioned, when they may isolate themselves or become as disruptive as a teenager, and during which the initiate's everyday life might be forcibly and painfully reshaped by the Gods. Part of the rite reveals the Dark Journey to the initiate, who is duly warned that he or she will have to tread this path, though until it has happened, they can have no concept of what is really means. Covens dread the time when members are coming up for their second degree because most of them go off the rails - a little or a lot – and can cause serious trouble in the meanwhile. The second degree candidate often seems to be regressing, rather than progressing, while the process takes place. Sadly, this is the flip side of people coming into their power. Egotism is always near to the surface in some individuals, in others it bubbles to the surface during the second degree process.

- Higher degrees are about advanced levels of spiritual and magical understanding and the candidate must demonstrate these skills to the HP and HPs.
- They must have achieved the maturity to be capable of acting as elders and assist in the running of the coven when called upon to do so.
- Second degree initiates must therefore be capable of leading religious rituals when called on to do so.
- The candidate must be capable of casting the circle and invoking the directions. This doesn't mean they must know the words and put on a convincing performance, it means that when they invoke, the call must be answered by spirit.
- They must be capable of raising the power within the circle.
- Candidates must demonstrate people skills, teaching skills and organisational ability.
- They must prove that they can put their own desires and egos aside for the benefit of others.
- They must be well balanced emotionally, psychologically and socially, able to relate to people at all levels of advancement.

The candidate is summoned to the edge of the circle and asked what they seek within this degree. Whereas in the first degree the candidate replied that they seek knowledge, in this degree the candidate responds that they seek "to better serve the Lord and Lady".

The first degree is about seeking knowledge, about learning, including the difficult job of learning about the self. In the second degree, this must have progressed to the point where the desire has become to serve – not because it makes the priest feel good, or makes people admire him, but because service to others is the way of the priest.

After first degree initiation, or after learning a healing skill, we all go through a stage where we want to shed our personal shiny new light on all and sundry. It makes us feel good to be considered a fount of knowledge, to be able to offer healing. People often go through a messianic stage, forcing 'good' on people whether they want it or not. It massages the ego of the doer very nicely and makes him feel useful and wonderful. Hopefully, the initiate or healer gains a level of maturity, and realises the gift must be used in a very different way.

Whatever happens in the circle is magnified in the ordinary world, whatever you place before the Gods at initiation will be reflected back to you many-fold. There is only one reason to seek higher degrees of initiation and that is to serve - the Gods and your fellow beings. It isn't to become important or to seek personal glory. Unless ego can be contained, the second degree will destroy the candidate. They start to believe they are something truly extraordinary, or the opposite happens and their ego is flattened.

The candidate is asked what they have done with their knowledge since the first degree, and have to be able to respond that they have guarded it from those who would profane it, have obeyed the elders and kept faith with their brothers and sisters in the coven, not betraying them and not speaking ill of them to others.

They are then reminded that before power is given an oath must be sworn and must reply that they will swear again what they have sworn before and ask the Lord and Lady to judge them and be their reward if they speak truthfully. If they are faithless, then they declare the Lord and Lady will turn from them, and if they are too daring – not ready – the Gods will destroy them. This is heavy stuff. If the candidate goes into the rite with ego to the fore, the Gods will ensure a long and painful process of stripping this away ensues, during which events will conspire to make sure that the Craft is denied to them.

The second degree ritual is based on the Dark Journey of the Goddess into the Underworld, and with her, the candidate travels and is forced to give up everything he thinks he has won until all that remains is an empty shell, ready to be filled with the true power of the Gods. This ritual reinforces the shedding of the ego – the candidate has been building himself up, gaining knowledge, power and prestige, and this degree shows him that his concept of this counts as nothing and must be sacrificed to take him to the next stage. In order to be reborn, one must die, and nothing won in this world can be carried into death. The death of the ego is not the death of the Self, but its birth. During the initiation ritual the candidate is stripped of his ego, his vision of himself and the world so as to allow the forces of the greater Cosmos to penetrate him.

Only then is the candidate remade with the power of the Gods. The high priest or priestess as initiator plugs in to the long established spiritual connection of the coven and the candidate experiences a down pouring of power, and thus the second degree initiation is performed. Unless the candidate is set, prepared and ready to receive and return the power, the initiation cannot take place. [1]

The results of second degree initiation are intense, and throw the new initiate off balance until the new world-view is assimilated. The initiate travels the Dark Road alone, and none can travel with him. He misses the easy knowledge-seeking of the first degree and feels resentment towards the initiator. He realises that the high priest and high priestess are like him- human beings with failings, undergoing their own journeys. The candidate often leaves the coven for a time, or for good.

1 There was an old belief that a witch could not die until she had passed on her power.

The second degree can fail for several reasons:

- If the initiate rejects what they have been given, and becomes bitter and angry
- If the candidate is not really ready for what is passed to them a mental breakdown can be the result.
- If the Gods reject the candidate and withhold the power

The Work of the Second Degree Initiate

- The work of the second degree is concerned with transcending ego in order to be able to participate fully in the group mind and group work. There are rituals and ceremonies which are only performed by second degrees and above. Hopefully, the initiate now enters the rite free of considerations of the material world, and transcends the barriers of the physical realm that separates us from the Cosmic Oneness, and his or her soul flies free. The neophyte and first degree still brings with them everyday considerations, and is trapped in physical existence, only able to glimpse at the distance the realms travelled by the advanced initiate.
- The focus of a second degree coven is high magic.
- The second degree learns to invoke the Gods into themselves, to channel the power of the Gods and speak with their voices. This is only achieved after forging contact and relationships with those Gods.
- To take a full and active part in the running of the coven and its affairs by participating in the Council of Elders [which consists of second and third degrees] who the High Priest/ess may call upon for advice. In certain circumstances, the elders may be called upon to judge and act in disciplinary matters.
- To teach the outer circles, probationers and neophytes as decided by the coven elders.
- The second-degree witch is given a new quest.
- A second degree can perform dedications and initiate up to first degree.

THIRD DEGREE INITIATION - HIGH PRIEST/ PRIESTESS

On completion of the second-degree quest, the third degree may be undertaken. At this level, the candidate becomes a high priest or priestess and can form their own Hearth if they wish. A person may spend twenty years in the Craft or even more before they are ready. To become a high priest or priestess, a person must wish to dedicate themselves to the Craft entirely, and be prepared to live the Craft before all else. During this ceremony, as in the second degree, the candidate calls down destruction on themselves if they are not worthy, swearing by their past lives and the future lives to come. No further quest is given at this stage.

The third degree involves the reconciliation of opposites, the marriage of God and Goddess on all levels of being, the child of this union being the true Self.[bn] The man must accept the Goddess within, and woman must accept the God within. Darkness and light must be recognised and accepted as one.

The Symbol:
The outward symbol of the third degree is the upright pentacle crowned by an upright triangle. This shows that the four elements are now in balance and crowned by the spirit, represented by the triangle of fire, the Cosmic spark, the higher soul.

The meditation symbol for third degree is the hexagram, which is composed of two fused triangles, one upward pointing, one downward. These two triangles represent polarities – the female and the male, water and fire, chalice and blade, night and day and so on. The candidate recognises that the two are reconciled in the One. To mark this, the third degree involves the Great Rite, the Sacred Marriage of the Goddess and the God in all its manifestations. This is done symbolically, unless an established couple are involved. The implication is that the initiate has facilitated this union within himself.

During this ritual, the initiator does not give power to the candidate, but facilitates them taking power to themselves. The third degree initiate takes the grade only in order to serve others. The person who takes it must not do so for his own glory, and must function in an unselfish way, putting the needs of the group first. A black cord is now worn, symbolising the defeat of the ego. Initiation takes place not from the west, the gate of death, but from the east, the gate of birth. Egyptian magicians [priests] were required to have the skill to enter and leave by the eastern doors of the sky i.e. able to travel the Cosmos in spirit.

THE FOURTH DEGREE

The fourth degree is rarely taken and very rarely achieved. The first part of the process involves the ultimate dissolution, and the second part complete restoration with the candidate open to the energies of the Cosmos in their proper manner and proper place.

COVEN HIVES

Coven hives are normally formed by a pair of third degrees who leave as high priest and priestess to form a new Hearth. In some circumstances, if they prove able and after they have gained enough experience of working as a second degree, the second-degree initiate may be given permission to form a coven hive i.e. to form their own coven and Hearth. In this instance, they then gain the title of High Priest/ess and are given permission to initiate to second degree.

With a hive, the Voiding the Coven rule comes into play. This states that the working grove and Outer Circle of the new coven must be a league [three miles] distant from those of the Mother Hearth. Furthermore, there should be no contact between the old coven and the new for at least a year. This seems rather odd and a bit cruel at first, but there are very good reasons for it. If the new Hearth is to forge its own identity it is necessary for it to be completely independent. A new High Priest/ess can't establish his/her authority if her members are continually running back to the old High Priest/ess for advice or just for a good moan. If a first or second degree witch leaves a coven for negative reasons they do not have the authority to found a new coven or initiate people in order to form a new coven. Only a third degree may do this.

Appendix 1
GLOSSARY

Athame – the ritual black handled knife
Cardinal points – north, south, east and west in the magic circle
Ceremony – from the Latin caerimonia, meaning an outward rite or observance, formal dignified acts on religious or public occasions. Often used synonymously with ritual.
Consecrate – literally 'to set aside' i.e. for sacred purposes
Curfane – the ritual white handled knife
Deosil – clockwise or sunwise
Elements – In Paganism this refers to earth, air, fire and water, and sometimes a fifth called spirit.
Guising – folk custom involving masks and fancy dress costumes
Left brain – the logical, rational, mathematical part of the brain
Libation – a liquid offering [e.g. wine] poured onto the ground
Macrocosm – The whole Cosmos, manifest and unmanifest, everything, all
Magick – Eliphas Levi first used the form 'magick' to differentiate religious or ceremonial magic from stage magic. In this he was followed by Aleister Crowley and others have added various other spellings such as majick and majic. Since we are talking about Pagan magic in this book, rather than Thelemic and other forms of ceremonial magic, I propose to stick to the conventional spelling.
Microcosm – the human being, and by extension, the human world. The microcosm is believed to be a reflection of the macrocosm.
Pantacle – the word used for pentagram in Thelema
Pentacle – used synonymously with pentagram but actually with a different etymology akin to pendant and pendulous i.e. an amulet hung from the neck.
Pentagram – a unicursal five pointed star
Pentalpha – the Pythagorean pentagram composed of five alphas.
Pentangle – a 1970s folk-rock band
Right brain – the artistic, creative and intuitive part of the brain
Ritual – from the Latin ritualis "relating to (religious) rites from ritus "a ceremonial act or series of acts, a prescribed method of procedure".
Sacrifice – literally 'to make sacred'
Sidhe – an Irish word for fairies
Talking stick – a stick or wand passed around a group with the proviso that only the person holding it may talk.
Wheel of the Year – the round of the festivals, especially the eight Sabbats.
Widdershins – anti-clockwise or anti-sunwise
Wildfolk – another word for the sidhe
Yule – the winter solstice

Appendix 2
HERBAL CORRESPONDENCES

EARTH:
Alfalfa
Barley
Bayberry
Bistort
Blackthorn
Briony
Buckwheat
Clover
Cypress
Elm
Fir
Fumitory
Hollyhock
Honeysuckle
Lilac
Mimosa,
Oakmoss
Patchouli
Pine
Primrose
Rhubarb
Sage
Soapwort
Sorrel
Strawberry
Tansy
Tonka
Tulip
Vervain
Vetivert

AIR:
Acacia
Agrimony
Alecost
Almond
Anise
Aspen
Bean
Benzoin
Bergamot
Carraway
Cedar
Celery,
Chervil
Chicory
Clary sage
Clover
Comfrey
Dandelion
Dill
Dock
Elecampane
Fenugreek
Fern
Hazel
Hop
Horehound
Houseleek
Lavender
Lemon verbena
Lily of the valley
Marjoram
Mint
Mistletoe
Mulberry
Niaouli
Nutmeg
Parsley
Pine
Sage
Sandalwood
Sweet Cicely
Sweet pea
Wormwood

FIRE:
Alder
Alexanders
Angelica
Asafoetida
Ash
Aspen
Avens
Basil
Bay
Betony
Cedar
Celandine
Centaury
Cinnamon
Cinquefoil
Clove
Clover
Cookoo pint
Coriander
Dill
Dragon's blood
Fennel
Flax
Frankincense
Galangal
Garlic
Gorse
Holly
Horsechestnut
Horseradish
Hyssop

Juniper
Lily of the valley
Lovage
Madder
Mandrake
Mustard
Nasturtium
Nettle
Oak
Olive
Peony
Rosemary
Rue
Saffron
Sassafras
Smallage
Sneezewort
St.john's wort
Sunflower
Tarragon
Vine
Walnut
Woodruff

WATER:
Aconite
Alder
Aloe
Apple
Ash
Balm [lemon]
Balm of gilead
Belladonna
Bindweed
Birch
Birthwort
Blackberry
Burdock
Camphor
Cardamon
Catnip
Cereus
Chamomile
Chervil
Cleavers
Clover
Coltsfoot
Columbine
Cornflower
Daisy
Damiana
Dog rose
Feverfew
Forget me not
Foxglove
Freesia,
Gardenia,
Geranium
Hellebore
Hemlock
Hemp
Henbane
Herb robert
Hyacinth,
Indigo
Ivy
Jasmine
Lady's mantle
Lily
Mallow
Marsh mallow
Meadowsweet
Melon,
Mugwort
Mullein
Myrrh
Myrtle
Narcissus,
Opium
Orris (iris)
Ox-eye daisy
Palmorosa
Periwinkle
Plumaria
Poppy (red)
Purslane
Rose
Rowan
Scullcap
Snowdrop
Spider lily
Stephanotis
Thyme
Valerian
Vanilla
Violet
Water lily
Willow
Woad
Wood aloe
Yarrow
Yew
Ylang ylang

Appendix 3
CHANTS, INVOCATIONS AND CHARGES

All chants and invocations © Anna Franklin unless otherwise stated.

CHANTS

The Earth is our Mother,
Our Father is the Sun
We dance with one another
And now the rite's begun.

Eko Eko Azarak, eko eko Zomelak, Eko Eko Cernunnos, Eko Eko Aradia
Traditional

Now about the circle go,
Ice and Water, ebb and flow
Earth is frozen, hard as stone,
Welcome Goddess, winter crone.

Thout a tout tout,
Through and about
In the Horned God's name!
Traditional

Lady bless thy secret child
My soul is true, my heart is wild

Twist ye, twine ye, even so
Mingle thread of joy and woe
Traditional Italian witch chant

Cummer, go ye before, cummer, go ye,
If ye willna go before, cummer, let me,
Ring-a-ring-a-widdershins
Linkin' lithely widdershins
Cummer carlin crone and queen
Roun' go we!

Cummer, go ye before, cummer, go ye,
If ye willna go before, cummer, let me,

Ring-a-ring-a-widdershins
Linkin' lithely widdershins
Kilted coats and fleeing hair
Three times three.

Cummer, go ye before, cummer, go ye,
If ye willna go before, cummer, let me,
Ring-a-ring-a-widdershins
Whirlin' skirlin' widdershins
And de'il take the hindmost
Who'er she be!

Traditional Scottish Witch Chant

INVOCATIONS

Invocation Of The Flower Bride

Lady of the flowers, come unto me
Lovely Blodeuwedd, I invoke thee
Formed of ninefold trees and ninefold flowers
Earth and magic and ninefold powers
From mountain primrose, bean and thorn,
From meadowsweet thou wast born,
From plants of light and plants of shade
From broom and thistle thou wast made.
Lady of the flowers come unto me.

Invocation of the Horned God

Horned Lord of the greenwood,
Spirit of the untamed places, thee I invoke.
Wild of heart, gentle and savage in turn,
Lord of Life and Lord of Death,
Descend we beseech thee, be with us tonight.

Invocation of the Goddess

Gentle Maiden, white armed lady of the moon,
Thee I invoke.
Fruitful Mother, full bellied with promise,
Thee I invoke.
Harvest Queen, life in your right hand, death in your left
Thee I invoke.

Cunning Hag, riding the hedges on your besom
Thee I invoke.
Come to us our Lady and Queen
And guide thy secret children.

Invocation of the Fairy Queen

Queen of Elphame, extend your milk white hand
Beringed with glistening drops of dew
Fairer than diamonds
And lead me into that Otherworld
That lies beyond the setting sun,
The western land, beneath the hollow hills
That open, when sun and season
Usher in Beltane and the summer,
And the slopes blaze with mortal fires.

Invocation of Brighid

Brighid, Exalted One, bright arrow of light
You arise like the shining sun in the east,
Born at sunrise, you shine amongst the stars of heaven
Your light has been extinguished and relit
We brave the darkness and light returns
You are the mother of the growing light
As a new cycle of life begins.
Yours are the three fiery arrows
You kindle creativity and regeneration
Woman of wisdom, adored by poets
Source of oracles, you give us seership and prophecy
Brigid the Smith,
Brighid the healer who imbues the holy wells with power
Golden-haired Goddess,
You give us plenty; you bring forth abundance from nature
You give us milk and grain

Invocation of Arianrhod

Arianrhod, starry Queen of the Northern skies,
Lady of Night, Lady of barren woodlands,
Lady of the crystal snows we call upon thee.
Mistress of Life, Mistress of Death,
Keeper of the Spiral Castle

Who guards the gateway of rebirth, we call upon thee.
Mother of the Light, we call upon thee,
Come and share our joy this night.

Invocation of the Harvest Goddess

Golden Goddess, whose hair is the waving yellow corn, crowned with poppies.
Golden Goddess, whose glorious harvest feeds us.
Descend I beseech thee and give blessing to thy children.

Charge of the Dark God

Harken to the words of the Horned One,
Whose names number more than the stars,
I am Herne, Cernunnos, Robin, Bel and Crom
I am the protector of all that lives upon the earth,
I am the dark hunter that men call Death.

Hear me, and let your heart leap at my summoning:
Listen for my voice in the wind, the whispering leaves,
In the roar of thunder across the midnight sky.
Leave behind the world of men and come to me,
Gather, my wild children, in the lonely places I love.

Look for me in the quiet heart of the forest,
In the bright fields of corn, the white light of the sun,
On the dappled river bank and the storm-savaged sea
I dwell in the centre of the labyrinth,
Beyond the grave in the Realm of Shadows

Be not afraid of my dark embrace
But surrender to it willingly,
And you will know the secrets beyond the tomb:
The light that dwells in darkness,
And my promise of knowledge, love and rebirth

Precious to me is the hot, bold spirit
The beloved fool that leaps, heedlessly
Into those unknown realms shunned by timid men
Only the wild at heart can know me,
For my face is hidden from the fearful

Come then, my wild children, and worship me.
Dance beneath the moon and call my name
I am Herne, Cernunnos, Robin, Bel, Crom
I am the protector of all that lives upon the earth,
I am the dark hunter that men call Death.

Charge of the Corn God
I am the plant of life,
Which comes forth from the God,
Which grows from the ribs of the God,
Which allows people to live,
Which makes the gods divine,
Which spiritualises the spirits,
Which sustains the masters of wealth and the masters of substance,
Which enlivens the limbs of the living.
I live as corn, the life of the living,
I live upon the God of the Earth,
But the love of me is in the sky, on earth, on the water and in the fields.
Now the Goddess is content, she rejoices for her son.
I am life appearing from the God.

INVOCATIONS OF THE DIRECTIONS

Spirits of the worlds above,
Realm of the Sky Gods
Arise and come unto us
Guardians of the worlds above, hail and welcome

Spirits of the worlds below,
Womb of the Goddess, realm of the dead and the unborn
Arise and come unto us
Guardians of the worlds below, hail and welcome

Guardians of the east,
Airy spirits of the winds
Arise and come unto us
Guardians of the east, hail and welcome

Guardians of the south
Burning spirits of the flame

Arise and come unto us
Guardians of the south, hail and welcome

Guardians of the west
Misty spirits of the waters
Arise and come unto us
Guardians of the west, hail and welcome

Guardians of the north
Elementals of the rich, moist soil
Arise and come unto us
Guardians of the north, hail and welcome

Lughnasa Hymn
Fields bright with corn,
Drenched with sun.
Lughnasa, beginning of the harvest.
The Mother, the Maiden are One.
In Hellenic garb Demeter and Persephone,
Or Brighid in all the Celtic lands,
Or Isis who watches over the fertilising Nile;
The Mother gives us bread, life-
Her arms seek to shelter us
Even in this age when we
Find it hard to se her face
In the dust of the modern world;
The technical jungle
Whose human seeds
May yet reunite us with the stars.
Where the Gods have always lived,
And from where they will come again-
As now, in glimpses in the woodland and plain,
Or where the seeing eye can look beyond
The dimness of the mind, the fettered logic
That never dares to dream, and find order again
In the pattern of Time and Space.
By Pamela Harvey[1]

---

1 *The Wellspring* by Anna Franklin and Pamela Harvey, Capall Bann,

John Barleycorn

The year did spin and spring come round
While our dear Lord lay in the ground
Till rain fell thick upon his bed
And slowly then he raised his head
And grew apace till Midsummer's Day
When with his flowering bride he lay
But the year spins round and he must die
And as a seed must once more lie
We hunt him down with sharpened sickle
To pierce his heart and see blood trickle
To flay his skin from off his bones
And grind him up between two stones
Our dying Lord has lost his head
But with his death we have our bread.

(Endnotes)

a http://www.rainewalker.com/book-page.htm

b Bill Whitcomb, The Magician's Reflection, Llewellyn, St Paul, 1999, p. xv

c W.E.Butler, Magic, Its Ritual Power and Purpose, quoted in The Ritual Magic Workbook by Dolores Ashcroft-Nowicki, The Aquarian Press, Wellingborough, 1986 p54

d Dion Fortune, Applied Magic, The Aquarian Press, Wellingborough, 1981

e Vivianne Crowley, Wicca, The Aquarian Press, Wellingborough, 1989

f Nigel Pennick, The Ancient Science of Geometry, Thames and Hudson, 1979

g John Michell, At the Centre of the World, Thames and Hudson, London, 1994

h Gracheva; G. K. Etnokulturnye kontakty narodov Sibiri. 1984, p 91

i Alexei Kondratiev, Samhain, Season of Death and Renewal, 1997

j John Michell, At the Centre of the World, Thames and Hudson, London, 1994

k ibid

l David Lewis Williams & David Pearce, The Neolithic Mind, Thames and Hudson Ltd, London, 2005

m ibid

n Murray Hope, The Psychology of Ritual, Element, Shaftsbury, 1988

o The Masks of the Goddess http://www.rainewalker.com/book-page.htm

p ibid

q ibid

r Nigel Pennick, Natural Magic, Lear Books,

s The Bacchæ, Euripides

t Nigel Pennick, Natural Magic, Lear Books,

u Aradia, The Gospel of the Witches, Charles Leland

v Euripides, Bacchae 135-150, trans. Philip Vellacott

w Nigel Pennick, Natural Magic, Lear Books

x ibid

y http://www.rainewalker.com/book-page.htm

z Quoted in The Art of Magic by Israel Regardie, Helios, 1969

aa Aleister Crowley, Magick in Theory and Practice, Chapter XIV

ab What the Bleep Do We Know, www.thebleep.co.uk

ac ibid

ad ibid

ae ibid

af ibid

ag Power of water

ah What the Bleep Do We Know, www.thebleep.co.uk

ai Christian Jacq, Magic and Mystery in Ancient Egypt, Souvenir Press, London, 1983

aj F.A.Yates, Giordano Bruno and the Hermetic Tradition, Routledge & Kegan Paul, London, 1964, p. 136

ak Christian Jacq, Magic and Mystery in Ancient Egypt, Souvenir Press, London, 1983

al ibid
am Richard Cavendish, The Magical Arts, Arkana, London, 1984,
an Carl Jung, Memories, Dreams and Reflections, Routledge & Kegan Paul, London, 1963
ao John Opsopaus, The Elements: Introduction © 1998
ap Anna Franklin, Personal Power, Capall Bann
aq John Opsopaus, The Elements: The Ancient Greek Esoteric Doctrine of the Elements, 1998
ar ibid
as ibid
at Paracelsus (1493-1541), Liber de nymphis, sylphis, pygmaeis et salamandris et caeteribus spiritibus.
au http://www.thelemapedia.org/index.php/Elements
av Krupps, Beyond the Blue Horizon
aw The Light of Britannia by Owen Morgan
ax ibid
ay Nigel Jackson, Compleat Vampire
az http://altreligion.about.com/library/weekly/aa121305a.htm
ba F. Marian McNeill, The Silver Bough, Cognate Classics, Edinburgh, n/d
bb Peter Beresford Ellis, Dictionary of Celtic Mythology, Constable, London, 1992
bc Ronald Hutton, Stations of the Sun, Oxford University Press, Oxford, 1996
bd David Clarke, A Guide to Britain's Pagan Heritage, Hale, 1995
be Samhain: Season of Death and Renewal Samhain by Alexei Kondratiev, 1997
bf ibid
bg "Welsh Folklore" by T. Gwynn Jones, Methuen and Co., London: 1930
bh Quoted in Mircea Eliade From Primitives to Zen, Collins, London, 1967, p 305
bi Dion Fortune, Applied Magic, The Aquarian Press, Wellingborough, 1981, p 28
bj Quoted in Mircea Eliade From Primitives to Zen, Collins, London, 1967, p 302
bk Quoted in Vivianne Crowley, Wicca, The Aquarian Press, Wellingborough, 1989
bl http://awardsideas.blogspot.com
bm Marija Gimbutas, The Language of the Goddess, Thames and Hudson, London, 1989
bn Vivienne Crowley, Wicca, The Aquarian Press, Wellingborough, 1989

NATURAL MAGIC

By Nigel Pennick

Natural magic is the way to work in harmony with the natural energies and forces that surround us all. Practising natural magic involves simple but effective practical techniques that all can use to become closer to the natural order of which we are all part. In this comprehensive introduction to natural magic, Nigel Pennick, author of 48 books on European traditional spirituality and folk-lore, provides us with an accessible in-depth approach to this most basic form of magic. The contents include an explanation of earth, mineral and plant magic; the magic of landscape and place; magical animals and how we can work with them; the power within the human body; natural magical charms, talismans and amulets, food and drink, and how to make and empower them.

"This is a welcome new edition with illustrations by the author. It teaches the reader how to work in harmony with the natural forces and elemental powers that surround us. It gives simple, yet effective, techniques to do this and many are based on the traditional witch ways known in east Anglia as the Nameless Arte...Highly recommended." Michael Howard, The Cauldron Magazine

£9.95 ISBN 0954475342-9

HEARTH WITCH

By Anna Franklin

Book one in the *Eight Paths of Magic Series*, this book is about walking the talk. The Hearth Witch sees the sacred within the physical, the magical in the mundane, and uses this knowledge to incorporate spiritual practice into her everyday life. The way of the Hearth Witch is an uncomplicated, direct form of magic, deceptively simple and unspeakably profound. A Hearth Witch is drawn to the traditional ways, the rhythms of nature and the call of the wildwoods. The Hearth Witch of today inherits the mantle of the village wise woman or cunning man. Hers are the Old Ways of the countryside, once passed down from mother to daughter, father to son, crone to apprentice. Herbs have always been part of the wise woman's armoury. A girl was initiated into the secrets of these family formulas by her mother, along with her knowledge of folklore, stories, healing potions, brewing and wine making, fortune telling and cookery know-how. Discover these secrets and the magic of the cunning woman in *Hearth Witch.*

"A surprising amount is packed into this volume - including the history, mythology, and folklore of the hearth witch. But mostly the book concerns the practical magic of the hearth. There are few "spells" here. Instead, there are recipes for seasonal dishes (all vegetarian), for incenses and dyes, for traditional natural toiletries and cleaning products. And there is advice on raising plants, storing and preserving produce, the uses of different woods, and candle making. Only a few generations ago, such knowledge was the inheritance of every woman. The traditional wise woman was also a master of the healing arts, and over a quarter of this book is devoted to "wort cunning" (or "knowledge of herbs" to use the more familiar Latinate words). The numerous ways of preparing herbs are explained, and a lengthy directory describes the uses of many common herbs. Necessarily this is only an introduction to the vast subject of herb lore, and the bibliography contains pointers to more in-depth studies (including Anna Franklin's own tome Herb Craft). All in all, this is an excellent source book for all 21st Century pagans, which I for one will be referring to time and again." Libra Aries

£11.95 ISBN 095475341-0

THE PATH OF THE

SHAMAN

By Anna Franklin

The Path of the Shaman is book two in Anna Franklin's *Eight Paths of Magic* series, exploring the role of the shaman, the mediator between the world of humankind and the world of spirits. This book explores, from the perspective of native British shamanism, the shamanic cosmos, the web of power, the shamanic crisis and becoming a shaman, healing and soul work, as well as working with the spirits of the land, plus animal and plant allies.

"I was moved beyond words by the beginning of this book. It reminded me of my traumatic numinous experiences which I have studiously tried to forget. It woke in me those vestiges of that path which I did not wish to traverse. I learned more, understood more and recognized more than I had before."
New Moon Reviews

£12.95 ISBN 0-9547534-4-5

For details and special offers visit www.learbooks.co.uk

THE NEW
PAGAN HANDBOOK
By Pat Regan

All ancient celebrations relate to Nature and humankind's place within the cosmic whole. Authentic Paganism is based on immutable truths. Unlike later man-made religions, Pagan worship is not in any way doctrinal but is a way of being. It is a great gift that we are all born with. The Old Gods reside deep within us; they dwell also in the vast uncharted corners of the universe and beyond. Their terrible yet beautiful force creates, destroys then creates anew all things in existence. The wondrous Lord and Lady of Paganism are as real today as they have ever been for those exceptional and enlightened people who welcome them into their hearts, minds and souls.

In *The New Pagan Handbook* Pat Regan explores the origins of Paganism, its suppression and re-emergence and looks at ways modern Pagans can express their faith and draw closer to the Old Gods. Using classical Roman Paganism as a model, this book shows you how to develop rituals and magic to suit your needs. With extensive appendices on symbolism and festivals, *The New Pagan Handbook* will help you to begin your own Pagan journey.

Pat Regan has worked for many years with the Pagan Anti-defamation Network (PAN), campaigning, researching and writing many articles on Paganism and ecology and is the author of *The Torch and the Spear*.

MIDSUMMER
By Anna Franklin

The celebration of Midsummer is a pan-global custom. Every culture has, at some point in its history, marked the time and held it to be enchanted. The Celts, the Norse and the Slavs believed that there were three 'spirit nights' in the year when magic abounded and the Otherworld was close. The first was Halloween, the second was May Eve and the third was Midsummer Eve. On this night, of all nights, fairies are most active. On this night the future can be uncovered. As the solstice sun rises on its day of greatest power it draws up with it the power of herbs, standing stones and crystals. In the shimmering heat haze on the horizon its magical energies are almost visible. And as the mist gate forms in the warm air rising beneath the dolmen arch the entrance to the Otherworld opens- Avalon, Tir nan Og, the land of Youth where it is *always* summer and death and old age are unknown. Shakespeare captured all the magic of the occasion in *A Midsummer Night's Dream* where fairies, magic and mischief abound on one bewitched night in the forest.

In this book, Anna Franklin explores the history and lore of Midsummer and offers rituals and methods of celebrating this ancient festival.

£12.95

LUGHNASA
By Anna Franklin & Paul Mason

Lughnasa is the neo-Pagan festival that celebrates the start of the harvest at the beginning of August. The name is Irish Gaelic and means the *násad* (games or an assembly) of Lugh, a leading Celtic deity and hero. The celebration supplanted earlier harvest festivals with older deities, and has themes which echo similar festivals in other parts of the world – the battle for the harvest, the end of summer growth and the sacrifice of the corn god.

Previously published as *Lammas*, this new edition contains material that was excised from the original book which examines the complex themes of Lughnasa and sacrifice. It also offers ideas on how to celebrate the festival with rituals, crafts and traditional Lughnasa games.

£12.95

For details and special offers visit www.learbooks.co.uk

HANDFASTING
By Anna Franklin

A handfasting is a Pagan wedding, usually the union of two individuals, perhaps two members of a coven or solo practitioners who meet and fall in love. The couple declare their love and commitment to each other, and promise that they will live together for a year and a day or *'for as long as love shall last'* in the words of one ritual. At the end of that time, they may renew their vows, make a more permanent commitment and a legal marriage, or go their separate ways. In an age when, for whatever reason, many relationships do not last a lifetime and divorce is commonplace, it is perhaps a sensible option.

Many Pagans think that it is very important for them to be able to declare their commitment to each other in a ritual that expresses their own beliefs, feeling that a secular ceremony is not as fulfilling and meaningful as the declaration of love before their gods and their peers. The vows are usually written by the couple themselves to express their own needs and emotions. A handfasting re-enacts the great Cosmic theme of the love of the Goddess and the God and the eternal verity of human love, recreated and renewed with every lover that exists or ever existed. The pair enter the circle as two separate people, and are transformed into a declared couple, a life changing event and an important rite of passage in life's journey.

Handfasting explores the origins and traditions of the custom with explanations and ideas for ritual, traditions and crafts to help you celebrate the occasion.

£12.95

For details and special offers visit www.learbooks.co.uk

BEYOND ILLUSIONS

By Deborah Sless

Why am I here? What is the purpose of my life? We all return to these questions in our quest for happiness and peace. And because each one of us is a unique individual, we look for the answers to these questions by setting off on our own unique journey. Along the way, we will find ourselves making changes to our lives, spurred on by our inner yearning for harmony. Some of these changes will be easier and quicker to make than others but, unless we keep on making them, our journey will shudder to a halt.

Psychotherapy provides us with the opportunity to change the inner structures that stop us being who we really are. These structures are often called adaptations and they came about in response to our childhood experiences of feeling threatened (for example, where we've felt physically unsafe or unsure that our needs would be met). When we build an adaptation, we change some of our inner structures. And, we hold on to them because we believe that our survival, and getting our needs met, depends upon doing so. The intention of our journey is to raise our level of awareness so we can gradually move away from our adaptations. When we can access and understand these adapted aspects of ourselves, we can start to make the deeper changes required to manifest and experience that which we truly desire.

£10.95